Homestyle
Puerto Rican Cooking

Traditional recipes with a modern touch!

Erisbelia Garriga

ISBN-0-9762088-0-6
1st. edition, November 2004
Cover: Chicken Asopao / *Asopao de Pollo*

Printed in Colombia, South America
Published by Casablanca Publishing, Inc., Atlanta, GA, USA

Homestyle
Puerto Rican Cooking

Traditional recipes with a modern touch!

Erisbelia Garriga

DEDICATION. . .

To my parents, Eufemia Illas and José M. Garriga, who sat
down and shared their recipes with me.

ACKNOWLEDGMENTS

To Julio, my youngest brother who for years was constantly asking when were we going to publish our family cookbook. To my husband, Manuel, for never saying no to all my requests, from proofreading the text to trying some of the dishes, for his support and valuable suggestions. To my immediate family, and friends who have contributed in one way or another to the completion of this project.

The following recipes were provided by other family members and a friend:

1. Cuajito - Gladys Illas-Morales
2. Pollo Asado con Jengibre – Maria Luisa Garriga
3. Bebidas – Aurelia Garriga
4. Mazamorra – Ana M. Villanueva
5. Dulce de Coco con Tomate – Carmen Meléndez
6. Parcharrón – Alberto Bonilla
7. Salsa de Mayonesa - Vanessa E. Garriga

We appreciate the kindness of Roberto Santana and Julio Viloria of "La Marqueta de Williamsburg" for allowing us to take pictures of some of the vegetables shown in this book. "La Marqueta de Williamsburg" is located at 108 Moore Street, Brooklyn, NY. Tel. 718-384-1371. (Photos were taken on May 7, 2003.)

Cover design: Liliana Gutiérrez
Typography: Julio Garriga
Photography: Edgar Solís
Proofreader: Manuel A. Ramos, PhD.
Photo on page 68 Courtesy of Jason Stemm, 2003

NOTE: Each recipe has the name in Spanish and English. The English term is only descriptive. In a restaurant it may help to order by the Spanish name.

5

TABLE OF CONTENTS

RECIPE LISTING

8

MAIN MEALS

MEAT

Introduction

Puerto Ricans have their roots in three ethnic groups: the Taino Indians, the original inhabitants of Puerto Rico, the Spanish who colonized the island in 1493, and the Africans who were brought to work on plantations as slaves. Over time Puerto Rico has also had the influence of others, such as French, Italian, and American.

This family cookbook will introduce the reader to our treasured classic Puerto Rican recipes as well as new ones. It is a collection of family recipes and the result of my experimentation with food. It is about innovation, taking simple ingredients and playing them off each other. The majority of the recipes are from my parents, others are personal and a few others from family members and friends. There are variations and familiar dishes were recreated, sometimes using substitute ingredients. Though family members, using the same ingredients, will prepare similar dishes in a different way, the end result is, nonetheless, a delicious, enjoyable dish.

Many of the recipes contain a number of ingredients, which can be substituted or omitted. I would suggest trying the recipe with all the ingredients it calls for the first time, even a second time, and thereafter add/reduce/omit those that you do not like or do not have, or cannot find in your grocery store. Before eliminating an ingredient, make sure you taste what you are cooking for that Spanish flavor. Sugar and salt are left to you to vary them according to taste. Most supermarkets, grocery stores or *bodegas* carry the ingredients found in this book. Look for the sign post that says *Spanish products*. With modern technology, anyone can order virtually any ingredient needed to prepare a special recipe using the internet. Check page 150 for sources where you can order special ingredients that cannot be found in supermarkets close to home.

Many varieties of tropical foods are associated with Puerto Rico. However, most of them were brought from other parts of the world. Some of our vegetables have different names, depending on the supermarket, the region of country you visit. Cooks may find that the same food item has a different name in another Spanish country. On page 82 there is a list with photos of the various root vegetables (tubers) that are used in the Puerto Rican cuisine. For those who are vegetarian, most of our Puerto Rican dishes will fit into their diets. Be creative by buying those products that are in season. They are fresher and will cost less than when bought off-season.

Puerto Ricans tend to cook for their immediate family and for "just in case" somebody else shows up for visiting. Here, we have tried to keep measurements of recipes for a minimum number of people: 4 to 6 persons. For most Puerto Ricans almost any occasion (e.g., wedding, graduation, a birthday, baptism and so on) is a reason to celebrate it with food and music. The kind of food served nowadays has changed during the last decade due to various factors; the economic situation, scarcity of some products, lack of cooking skills in the new generation, American fast food influence, and for some people cooking can be a chore rather than a pleasure.

When we visited another town or go to the beach, my mother would prepare *arroz con pollo* and red beans with a salad. She would get up at 4 or 5 in the morning to cook the food that we would eat for lunch or as soon as we felt hungry. We would stop along the road, under a shady tree to have our picnic lunch.

I remember the days when the whole family used to go to the country to celebrate the Christmas Season with *parrandas*, in which a group of friends and relatives who would "crash" into your home with music and singing Puerto Rican Christmas carols (*aguinaldos, villancicos*) without announcing themselves. They would go from house to house for an hour or two, and would always be welcome at any household. The only thing that host had to do was to provide food and drinks: *pasteles, arroz con gandules, asopao de gandules* or *de pollo, cuchifritos, lechón asado, pernil, morcillas, longanizas, almojábanas, dulce de coco, arroz con coco, coquito, cerveza fría, ron,* (some houses used to have a clandestine rum called *cañita*). Since many in the *parrandas* would go over the top drinking, coffee or hot chocolate would be served with soda crackers, *queso de bola holandés* (cheese), and the *asopao* (a thick rice soup) to lessen the effects of alcohol.

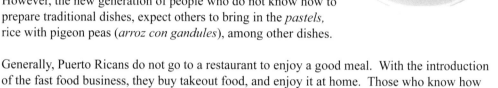

The music and food would make people feel festive, have a good time and enjoy the chance to wish everyone a merry Christmas and a happy new year. Today, things have changed somewhat. However, the new generation of people who do not know how to prepare traditional dishes, expect others to bring in the *pastels,* rice with pigeon peas (*arroz con gandules*), among other dishes.

Generally, Puerto Ricans do not go to a restaurant to enjoy a good meal. With the introduction of the fast food business, they buy takeout food, and enjoy it at home. Those who know how to cook prepare the meals for all the family at home for all to enjoy and are proud of their cooking skills.

Today with the help of a food processor and other labor-saving helpful kitchen devices, the recipes in this cookbook are very easy to prepare, cutting down on time. Some of these dishes can be prepared a day or two before you plan to serve them, especially the seasoning of meats or marinating fish as part of the process.

In the past, cooks used to simmer succulent meats and vegetables in a large iron kettle over an open hearth, ready to provide nourishment for the hard-working family. For lunch, Puerto Ricans on the island served vegetables, *viandas*, soups, aside from rice and beans. That has changed somewhat: nowadays, soups and *asopaos* (and sandwiches) are served as part of their lunch.

Puerto Ricans have learned to serve their dishes, which were part of a main course, as *hors d'oeuvres* in various social occasions, from casual to formal. *Hors d'oeuvres* are served for many to introduce dinner, or evening entertaining, as a complete buffet meal, or at receptions and banquets. Best of all, almost any food--fruits, vegetables, meats, cheese, small salads, and relishes—works as appetizer fare. So today, when going to certain places, *empanadillas de yuca, alcapurrias, bacalaítos, cuchifritos, guineos en escabeche, mollejas en escabeche, yuca al mojo,* among others, are often served as *hors d'oeuvres*.

Most people today are conscious about healthy eating habits. Food is planned based on nourishment, appeal, and preventing weight gain. The majority of the recipes here can be prepared using less fat, salt, and sugar. Be cautious with seasonings, herbs and spices, as using too much of them can overwhelm a dish. Puerto Rican food is very tasty and *sofrito* is the base ingredient for its seasoning. Though it tastes fresher when it is prepared at home, nowadays sofrito is sold at supermarkets, with the newest brand being sold in New York, *Sofrito y Recaito Al Estilo Puerto Rico. P*age 25 illustrates the main *sofrito* ingredients.

I have adapted dessert recipes from our diverse cultural heritage, allowed for variety with the aim of recapturing certain traditional sweets: *dulce de coco, tembleque, mazamorra, flan, arroz con coco, dulce de papalla, budines,* among others. They are all simple to prepare and can be prepared ahead of time.

12

There is a new generation of Puerto Rican cooks adding or experimenting with new flavors. They are revolutionizing our cooking using different ingredients, making it more practical in terms of finding the products and using what is available. One example is *Abuela's Pique*, a hot sauce, in five different flavors. Again, products and ingredients easy to find in supermarkets, specialty stores and the internet.

One example is the mango, originally from southeastern Asia, India and the Philippines. In the 18th Century it was brought to the Americas: first to Brazil, then Cuba, Mexico, Puerto Rico and other Antilles. It is said that today mango is the most widely eaten fruit worldwide. In Puerto Rico there are a number of mango varieties and are used in different ways: for sauces/syrups, ice cream, dessert, jelly, custard (*flan*), cakes, salads, and beverage/juices, among others. Similarly so with pineapple, oranges, sugar cane, yams and others, which are not native to Puerto Rico.

¡*Buen provecho*! *Bon appétit* as you try these recipes. . .

Ditas y Coquito

During my grandmother's time, "ditas" and "coquitos" were used in the kitchen. "Dita," a type of bowl, made from the güira (calabash) tree, was used to measure and pick through rice. Some Puerto Ricans may know it as "higüeras."

"Coquito," a cup made from the hard inner shell of the coconut, was used for drinking coffee.

Tips & Hints...

METRIC CONVERSION TABLE

Liquid and dry food cup and tablespoon measurements
(based on an 8 oz. cup)

2 cups equals one pint (16 oz.)			488 gr.
4 cups equals one quart			0.95 ml
1 cup equals 8 fluid ounces			250 milliliter (ml)
3/4 cup	=	12 tbsp	190 ml
1/2 cup	=	8 tbsp	125 ml
1/3 cup	=	5.3 tbsp	80 ml
1/4 cup	=	4 tbsp	60 ml
3 tsp	=	1 tbsp	15 ml
1 tsp	=	1/3 tbsp/60 drops	5 ml
1/2 tsp	=		3 ml
1/4 tsp	=		1.5 ml
pinch or dash	=	less than 1/8 teaspoon	

WEIGHT / VOLUMEN

16 oz	=	1 pound	= 500 grams
8 oz	=	1/2 lb.	= 250 grams
4 oz	=	1/4 lb	= 125 grams
1 oz	=		= 30 grams

TEMPERATURE

F		C
400	=	200
350	=	180
325	=	160
300	=	150
275	=	140
250	=	120
200	=	100

Kitchen Equipment

In our kitchen you will find standard pans, skillets and baking dishes to prepare any of the recipes on this book. However, there are some utensils that can make the cook's life easier: double-boiler (*baño de María*), mortar and pestle (*pilón y maceta*), *tostonera*, grater (*guayo-rayador*), a food processor, a blender, and *calderos*. I find that rice cooks better in a *caldero* than in any other standard cooking pan.

tostonera

grater

mortar and pestle

caldero

Food Processor

Double boiler

Blender

Table Setting...

For most meals, a five-piece setting is adequate: fork, knife, table-spoon, teaspoon, and small fork.

Some tips before starting to cook

Read the selected recipe carefully and bear in mind that:

      1   all the ingredients are on hand
      2   all ingredients are measured
      3   all needed cooking utensils are on hand

The following tips are useful should something happen during the cooking process:

1. If the grains (say, beans), soups or stews are too salty, drop in a potato or two to absorb the salt. Discard the potato once the desired taste has been reached.

2. If the liquid for the beans/grains doesn't thicken, use potatoes, pumpkin or a little starch. If stew results too greasy, add Roman lettuce leaves to absorb fat.

3. When boiling tubers or pasta, drop a clove or two of garlic in the water for extra flavor.

4. When preparing stock for soups, sancochos, stews or sauces, use the stock from boiled bones or vegetables. This same stock is also usable for rice or pasta.

5. When handling green bananas or plantains, cut the ends and drop them in salted water to prevent discoloring and stickiness on the fingers and hands. Some cooks prefer rubber gloves.

6. If the rice smell smoked or burnt when cooking, drop some onion slices on top of the rice and cover. Bread slices can achieve the same purpose. Discard said items before serving rice.

7. If the saltiness of salted codfish isn't reduced on the first go round, add some sugar to the water and re-boil. (Salted codfish should be desalted by the boiling at least twice.)

8. To keep broccoli nice and green, add a teaspoon of baking soda if cooking in water.

9. To maintain the whiteness of cauliflower, add some milk to the water while cooking.

10. If certain dessert recipes call for raisins, lightly dredge them in flour before adding to the mix to prevent them from sinking to the bottom during the cooking process.

11. To obtain the maximum juice from a lemon, try cutting it length-wise rather than at the mid-point. (Some cooks prefer "rolling" the lemon over a flat surface with the palm of the hand and then cut in halves).

12. When using an avocado, sprinkle with lemon or leave the seed inside so that it will not darken.

13. After handling fish, wash hands with some lemon juice to avoid the fishy smell.

14. When cooking fish whole, add a slice or two of lemon or orange inside the fish head for extra flavor.

15. When handling very hot chiles, use rubber gloves and avoid touching sensitive areas, such as the eyes or nose.

16. Almost all vegetables and tubers should be washed before cooking. (There are special brushes for that purpose, if desired.)

17. When a recipe calls for beaten eggs, they should be at room temperature. The bowl for the whisking must be completely clean. When there aren't enough eggs to prepare an omelet, add some heavy cream in the mix for volume.

18. To determine if a fresh coconut is unspoiled, shake it close to the ears to hear if the water inside swishes about. If it does, it's safe to say the coconut is good

19. When handling wines, most reds should be at room temperature. Whites should be chilled (but not ice-cold as with beers).

20. When cooking with wine, it should be the type one would serve at the table.

21. When cutting meats, use a separate cutting board for fowl, other meats and vegetables.

22. When preparing meats, season and refrigerate until ready to cook.

23. If a greased skillet catches fire, turn off the stove and spread baking powder or baking soda over the fire.

Suggestions for leftovers

Be creative with leftovers. Here are some possibilities:

- Make a chili con carne if there are extra red beans leftover.

- Use leftover groundmeat as a filling for baked peppers or chayotes, potato or yucca balls, meatballs, or for any recipe calling for groundmeat, including pasta.

- Use leftover crabmeat stew as a filling for alcapurrias, stuffed plaintains and other fritters.

- Use leftover white rice to create a vegetarian dish, using assorted vegetables. Leftover steak can be cut in small pieces and added to white rice plus a few extra vegetables for a stir fry. Leftover bell peppers can be used for salads.

- Leftover roast chicken can be converted into a nice chicken salad, as part of a stir-fry, for a tortilla (omelet) or for sandwiches. Same with turkey.

- The liquid from boiled vegetables can serve as a base for soups, consommés, stocks and the like.

- A tortilla (omelet) can be made from leftover fries, by cutting them up into small pieces, crushed garlic, some sofrito, beaten eggs, salt and pepper to taste.

- Leftover codfish can be shredded and used to make codfish fritters, for salads and even with rice. It's great in an eggplant stew.

- Use extra fruits leftover in a salad, for shakes, or to garnish desserts.

- Leftover cooked (sauceless) grains can be used for salads.

- Meat bones and fish heads are good for making flavorful stocks and may be frozen for later use. Small containers would be helpful for that.

- Leftover bread can be used for making bread pudding; toasted and cubed for salads; as bread crumbs for dredging; as a substitute for the gram cracker base for some cheesecakes; or in toasted slices for bruschettas, using seasoned diced tomatoes with cilantro.

- Leftover (strong) coffee can be used in preparing a dessert-lady fingers custard cake, in some flans or even hot chocolate.

- Extra hard-boiled eggs can serve as a filling, for salads, and with sautéd codfish.

- Cheese: If creamy, use it to prepare mashed potato or for filling other dishes If hard, cut in small pieces or grate it for salads and omelets.

RECOMMENDED STORAGE TIMES FOR SOME FOOD PRODUCTS

According to the University of Georgia Cooperative Extension Service and the Georgia Department of Agriculture "freezing is an excellent way to preserve animal products such as meat, poultry, fish and shellfish. . . Freezing affects the texture, color, juiciness and flavor of foods. . . Once the food is frozen, it should be kept at 0 degree F or below. " Once meats are brought home, clean, wash, and season them immediately. Avoid leaving them at room temperature for more than two hours.

They also point out that "cured meats such as ham and bacon can only be frozen for a short period of time (1 to 3 months) because the salt in them hastens rancidity."

They also suggest that when using spices, use them in a small quantity before freezing certain foods. Add more seasoning when ready to cook. When freezing food, label all packages with the date and type of food. Cut meats in meal-size portions before freezing them.

Regarding storage times, nutritionists at the University of Georgia recommend:

FOOD ITEM	STORAGE PERIOD
Margarine	9 months
Cheese	
dry-curd cottage cheese, ricotta	2 weeks
natural, process	3 months
Cream (all kinds)	2 months
Whipped	1 month
Egg whites or yolks	1 year
fatty fish	3 months
lean fish	6 months
shellfish	3 months
Ice cream/sherbet	1 month
Meat	
bacon	1 month
frankfurters	2 months
ground or stew meat	3 months
ham	2 months
roasts	
beef or lamb	1 year
pork or veal	8 months

```
steak or chops
        beef ..................................................................... 1 year
        lamb or veal ..................................................... 9 months
        pork ................................................................. 4 months
    variety meats ......................................................... 4 months
Milk  ................................................................ 1 to 3 months
Poultry
        cooked, with gravy ............................................. 6 months
        cooked, no gravy ................................................ 1 month
        uncooked (whole chicken/turkey) ......................... 1 year
        duck or goose .................................................... 6 months
        uncooked (parts)
            chicken  ....................................................... 9 months
            turkey  ......................................................... 6 months
  Yogurt
        plain  ............................................................... 1 month
        flavored  .......................................................... 5 months
```

They recommend that when a range is given, to use the shorter storage time for best quality. And after the storage periods, the food is still safe but lower in quality.)

_____

Source: University of Georgia Cooperative Extension Service, College of Family and Consumer Sciences in cooperation with the College of Agricultural and Environmental Sciences, "Preserving Food: Freezing Animal Products". Received from the Georgia Department of Agriculture, August 2003.

Sofrito

Ingredients:

3 garlic heads
2 medium-size onions
1 green bell pepper, seedless
1 large size tomato
1 tsp oregano leaves
12 small sweet peppers,
   seedless (ajíes dulces)
15 to 20 cilantro/cilantrillo stems (ramitas)
15 to 20 culantro/recao leaves
10 to 15 olives (pitted)
1 tablespoon of capers

Procedure:

1. Wash thoroughly the cilantro and recao.
2. In a blender or food processor, mix all ingredients to a coarse puree. Store in an ice-cube tray and freeze. Use one or two cubes when cooking soups, stews, and or seasoning meats.

Notes:

The olives and capers can be substituted for "Alcaparrado" which has the olives stuffed with red peppers and capers. Add some of the liquid to the mixture. Peel garlic and onions. Remove seeds from peppers. Mix all of ingredients in a mixer (blender or food processor). Chop coarsely. You can use an ice cube tray and pour the mix. (Every time you cook something that needs sofrito, take an ice cube and use in your cooking.)

If you are using a blender, probably you need to add water. Instead of water, I recommend blending first one or two tomatoes, some of the liquid of the capers and olives, which will give a better taste to the "sofrito." If using a food processor, its not necessary to add any liquids, however, it is recommended that you add these liquids for a tastier sofrito.

---

* For most people in Puerto Rico, cilantro is interchangeable for recao. However, in some farmer's markets "recao" goes by the name of "Thai Culantro".

Main Ingredients for Sofrito

Garlic (ajo)

Sweet Pepper

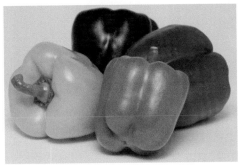

Bell Peppers (Pimientos)

Onions (Cebollas)

"Recao / Culantro"

Tomatoes

Oregano

Cilantro

25

Flavor Enhancers

In addition to the sofrito/recaíto, and powder adobo, the three ingredients below will also provide that special Spanish flavor: tocino (salt pork), cooking ham and ham hocks.

 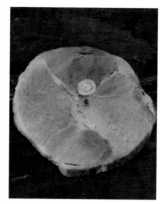 

Salt Pork (Tocino)   *Cooking Ham (Jamón)*   *Ham Hocks (Patitas de cerdo ahumadas)*

Food Coloring...

Color in stews and rice can be enhanced by using one of the following

Tomato Sauce   *Saffron*   *Annatto Seasoning*   *Paprika*

Annatto seed (achiote), oil, and annatto oil

To prepare annatto oil:

2 tablespoons of annatto seeds   •   1 cup of cooking oil

Mix the two ingredients and let cook for two or three minutes until oil takes on a reddish color. Strain.

Appetizers

Puerto Rican families have become more creative and serve dishes--once part of the main course--as appetizers and hors d'oeuvres. They eat these at any time as snacks, lunch, dinner, and even for breakfast. They are nice starters to dinner, evening entertaining, as a complete buffet meal on casual and formal occasions.

Almost any food, including fruits, vegetables, meats, cheese, small salads, can serve as an appetizer. Today, *empanadillas de yuca, alcapurrias, bacalaítos, cuchifritos, guineos en escabeche, mollejas en escabeche, yuca al mojo*, among others, are served as appetizers as a well as a main course. With today's dieting concerns, they are generally served in small sizes.

Avocado Dip

Mojo de Aguacate
(10-12 servings)

Ingredients:

2 ripe avocados
1 small ripe tomato
3 cilantro leaves finely chopped
½ small grated onion
1 tsp olive oil

1 tbsp lemon juice
2 tbsp sofrito
2 garlic cloves, mashed
salt & pepper to taste

Procedure:

1. Cut the avocados in halves and using a spoon scoop the pulp into a deep bowl.
2. Add onion, tomato, sofrito, garlic, salt and pepper and mix well.
3. Using a fork, mash all the ingredients together.
4. Add the lemon juice, chopped cilantro and taste for salt.

Serve with chips, pita bread or raw vegetables, such as broccoli, cauliflower, celery stalks or carrots.

Chickpeas Dip
Mojo de Garbanzos
(8-10 servings)

Ingredients:

1 lb chickpeas, cooked
2/3 cup Tahini sauce
   (crushed sesame seeds)
2 tbsp lemon juice
½ tsp vinager
2 tsp olive oil

1 tbsp sofrito
4 cloves garlic, finely mashed
½ tsp adobo, powder
½ tsp black pepper, ground
½ tsp ground cummin
½ tsp paprika
2 cilantrillo leaves, minced

Procedure:

1. If using fresh chickpeas, leave them in water overnight. The following day, change the water. Boil them in four cups of fresh water, a bay leaf, one clove of garlic, half a chicken bouillon cube, and a pinch of salt until tender, approximately one hour. Reserve some of the liquid to smooth the blend. (Otherwise skip this step by using one can of chickpeas.)
2. In a blender or food processor, combine all ingredients, (except paprika and cilantrillo leaves, which will be used to garnish).
3. Serve in dip platter. Sprinkle with paprika and cilantrillo.

Serve with warm pita bread or raw, crunchy vegetables such as broccoli, cauliflower, celery.

Note: *This dip can be used as a seasoning for salads or sandwiches.*

Spinach Dip
Mojo de Espinaca
(25 servings)

Ingredients:

1 bag fresh spinach
5 or 6 culantro leaves
2 cloves garlic
1 tsp adobo
1 cup sour cream
½ pkg garlic cheese (spread)

1/2 pkg of cream cheese
1/2 celery stem
1 small onion
2 pkg of chicken broth (powder)
1 can of water chestnuts (drained)

Procedure:

1. Wash, pat dry spinach.
2. Mix all ingredients in a food processor. Taste (The adobo and chicken broth are salty. Add salt only if needed.)

Serve with crackers, vegetables or chips.

Note: Organic spinach is better though often a bit more expensive.

Rice Fritters
Almojábanas
(15 fritters)

Ingredients:

2 cups rice flour

1 tsp salt

2 tbsp butter

vegetable oil for frying

1 cup fresh milk

2 jumbo eggs

¾ cup grated parmesan cheese

Procedure:

1. Using a sifter, mix rice flour and salt.
2. Melt butter and add to flour mix.
3. Boil milk and add little by little to flour mix until it is moistened. (If mix is still dry, add more milk.) Stir and let it cool.
4. Add eggs one at a time to the mix, stirring well after each addition.
5. Add cheese and mix together.
6. To fry, drop tablespoon portions of batter into hot oil and fry until light brown. Drain fritters on paper towel.

Serve with hot chocolate or coffee.

Codfish Fritters
Bacalaítos
(15 – 20 fritters)

Ingredients:

1 lb codfish, boneless
2 cups water
2 cups all purpose flour

1 tsp baking powder
1 envelope sazón con achiote
1 tsp adobo
1 tbsp olive oil with achiote

2 tbsp sofrito
2 garlic cloves, mashed
5-6 cilantro and recao leaves,
    finely minced
1 tsp oregano
1 egg
salt and pepper to taste
frying oil

Procedure:

1. Desalt codfish: Leave in water for at least two hours. Change water. Then boil in water for ten minutes. (Reserve two cups of this water to moisten flour.) If codfish is still too salty, add 3-tablespoons sugar to water and boil again. Taste.
2. Remove codfish from water and shred in small pieces removing skin and any bones. Set aside.
3. In a large bowl, sift together all dry ingredients. Add sofrito, garlic and cilantro, recao, orégano, egg, and mix well.
4. Add one cup of reserved water and stir until flour is moistened. If mixture is too thick, add more water.
5. Add codfish and stir. Taste for salt and pepper.
6. Using a deep frying pan, drop teaspoons or tablespoons of mixture to hot oil, and fry until lightly browned. Drain on absorbent paper towel.

Best served hot. They go well as appetizers or as a side dish.

Corn Fritters

Arepitas
(20 – 25 arepitas)

Ingredients:

2 cups cornmeal

1 pinch salt

¼ cup sugar

1 tsp baking powder

1 ½ cups milk, hot

2 tbsp melted butter

2 large eggs

frying oil

Procedure:

1. Sift together cornmeal, salt, sugar and baking powder in a large bowl.
2. Add hot milk to moisten flour mix. Stir. (If it's not completely moistened, add more hot milk.)
3. Add butter. Stir and let cool a minute or so.
4. Add eggs and stir well.
5. Fry by dropping teaspoons of mixture into hot oil, until lightly browned. Remove and drain on paper towel.

Serve alone with hot chocolate or coffee.

Note: Almojábanas de maíz, a variety of corn fritters can be prepared by adding a 3/4 cup grated permesan cheese.

Corn Sticks Fritters

Surullos
(20-30 sorullos)

Ingredients:

1 ½ cup cornmeal	2 tbsp butter
1 tsp baking powder	½ cup parmesan cheese
½ tsp salt	¼ lb cheddar cheese
1 cup water	½ cup flour
	2 cups frying oil

Procedure:

1. Sift cornmeal and baking powder. Add salt and parmesan cheese.
2. Boil water and butter and add to the cornmeal mixture. Stir well. Let cool for 10 minutes
3. In the meantime, cut cheddar cheeses in julienne strips 1/8 thick and set aside.
4. Sprinkle your hands with flour. Place a tablespoon of cornmeal mixture in your hands. Put a strip of cheese in the center and cover with mixture, by rolling the mixture in your hands shaping it into cylindrical form.
5. In a frying pan, heat oil over high heat. Fry *surullos* until golden brown on both sides. Drain on paper towel.

Best served hot, along with coffee, hot chocolate or tea.

Fried Plantains with Garlic Sauce
Tostones con Salsa de Ajo
(4 or 5 servings per plantain)

Ingredients:

4 green plantains
3 cups water
2 tbsp salt

4 –5 cloves garlic, finely smashed
1 cup frying oil

Procedure:

1. In a large bowl, prepare water with salt and two cloves of garlic.
2. Peel plantains, and cut into one-inch thick, diagonal slices. Soak for 10 minutes in water with salt and garlic. Drain well.
3. In a deep skillet, heat oil for two or three minutes until very hot, add plantain slices and fry until light brown on both sides. Remove and place on absorbent paper towel.
4. If there is no"tostonera", use the plantains peelings to flatten the plantain slices with the heel of the hand until about ¾ their original thickness.

Continued on next page

5. Soak the flattened slices in the salted water and remove immediately. Drain and fry again until crips and golden. (Watch for splattering.) Drain on paper towel.
6. Prepare a sauce by combining the remaining mashed garlic and olive oil. Mix well. with a kitchen brush coat mixture over the plantain slices. Light salting optional.

Serve immediately

Note: ***Tostones are easy to prepare using a tostonera, a kitchen gadget made of two pieces of wood. Now a new tostonera with a small bowl space in the center can be found at some Spanish markets. Great for preparing stuffed fried plantains.***

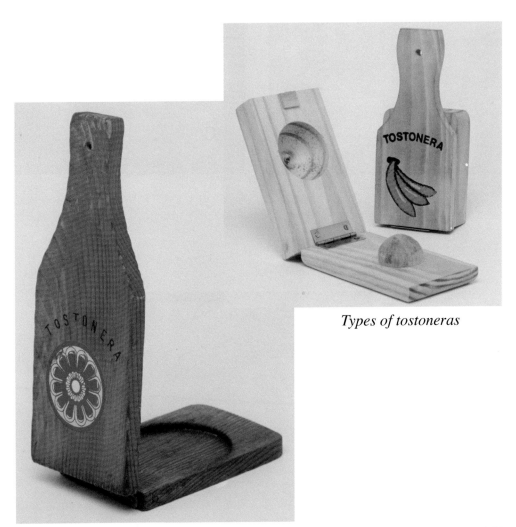

Types of tostoneras

Peeling a Plantain...

1. Cut the end tips of the plantain.

2. Gripping one end with fingers, with a knife cut a slit along the length of the plantain through the skin.

3. Using a spoon or a round-end knife, pry off the skin by slipping it between the peel and the plantain.

4. Using a cutting knife, slice plantain diagonally into pieces ½ to ¾-inch thick.

Plantain slices

Fried Ripe Bananas
Caballitos
(5 servings)

Ingredients:

1 ½ cup all-purpose flour
1 pinch salt
5 ripe bananas

1 cup water
1 tsp baking powder
1-cup frying oil or 1 butter stick

Procedure:

1. Peel and cut bananas lengthwise, then in halves.
2. Mix flour, salt and baking powder with water.
3. Dredge bananas in flour mixture.
4. Fry in hot oil or butter. Drain in paper towel.

Serve hot as a side dish or appetizer.

Stuffed Plantain Fritters

Alcapurrias
(about 10 Fritters)

Ingredients:

4 green plantains
4 cups water
1 lb ground meat
1 tsp adobo
3 tbsp sofrito
½ cup tomato sauce

1 tbsp stuffed olives
1 lb yautía
1 small jar red peppers
salt & pepper to taste
1/4 cup flour
2 tbsp olive oil with achiote
frying oil

Materials: One or two banana leaves

Procedure:

1. Cut ends of plantains and place in salted water for two or three minutes. Peel and leave in salted water until ready to be grated.
2. In a medium saucepan, sauté meat. Add sofrito, tomato sauce, adobo, water, olives and red peppers. Continue cooking until meat is browned. Taste for salt and pepper. Stir and set aside.
3. In a separate large pan, finely grate plantains and yautía. Add one fourth cup of flour, adobo, and one-teaspoon olive oil with achiote. Mix well using your hands. Set aside.

Continued on next page

4. Place one tablespoon of plantain mixture on a banana leaf and spread it with the same tablespoon.
5. Place one-tablespoon meat on the plantain mix, spread and cover by folding the plantain leaf, to form a cylindrical shape. Remove from banana leaf, and place in a flour-powdered dish.
6. Deep fry in hot oil, until brown for both sides. Oil must be very hot and should cover fritter. Remove and drain on absorbent paper.

Best served hot. If used as an appetizer, leave frying until guests arrive.

Note: If banana leaves are not available, use aluminum foil. Oil should be very hot. If there is no hot oil thermometer, drop a cube of bread into oil, if oil bubbles and bread cube quickly browns, the temperature is just right.

Ñame Fritters
Buñuelos de Ñame
(10 – 12 buñuelos)

Ingredients:

2 lb ñame
¼ tsp baking powder
½ tsp salt

½ tsp adobo
2 cups frying oil

Procedure:

1. Peel, wash, and grate ñame.
2. Add baking powder, salt and adobo. Hand beat for three minutes until mixture is smooth.
3. Drop tablespoon of mixture in hot oil and fry until lightly browned.
4. Drain on paper towel.

Best served hot.

Yautía Fritters
Buñuelos de Yautía
(15 – 20 buñuelos)

Ingredients:

2 lb yautía
2 tbsp adobo
1 tbsp sofrito
½ tsp baking powder

salt to taste
1 large egg
2 cups frying oil

Procedure:

1. Peel, wash and grate yautía.
2. Add adobo, sofrito, baking powder and salt, and mix well. Taste for salt.
3. Add egg and mix well.
4. Place oil in a deep frying pan at high heat until is very hot.
5. Drop tablespoons of the mixture, and fry until light brown on both sides. Place in paper towels.

Best served hot as an appetizer or a side dish.

Yucca Fritters

Almojábanas de Yuca

(15 fritters)

Ingredients:

1 cup yucca flour
1 adobo envelope
4 or 5 cilantro leaves finely chopped
2 tbsp butter
salt to taste

1 cup fresh milk
2 jumbo eggs
¾ cup grated parmesan cheese
vegetable oil for frying

Procedure:

1. Using a sifter, mix yuca flour and salt. Add adobo envelope and mix.
2. Melt butter and add to flour mix.
3. Boil milk. Add little by little to flour mix until is moistened. (If mix is too thick, add more milk.) Stir and let it cool.
4. Add eggs one at a time to the mix and stir well after each addition.
5. Add cheese and mix together.
6. To fry drop tablespoon portions of batter into hot oil and fry until light brown. Drain fritters on paper towel.

They go nicely with hot chocolate or coffee.

Cuajito
(5 servings)

Ingredients:

1 –1 lb cuajo (1 package)
½ green bell pepper, minced
1 small jar red peppers
6 stuffed olives
1 tsp small capers
¼ cup tomato sauce
½ cup cooking wine
1 medium tomato, cubed
1 tsp hot red sauce
1 tbsp olive oil w/achiote
juice of one lemon

2 medium potatoes, diced
1 parsley leaf, minced
3-4 cilantro leaves, minced
1 envelope sazón w/achiote
5 garlic cloves, mashed
1 tsp oregano
1 small onion, sliced
1 tsp adobo
½ tsp ground black pepper
½ tsp sweet basil
salt to taste

Procedure:

1. Wash, remove fat and cut "cuajo" in small pieces of approximately 2 inches. Rinse generously with lemon juice.
2. Season with black pepper, orégano, parsley, adobo and a pinch of salt.
3. Boil until tender, about 1-½ hours, with two garlic cloves, cilantro and half onion.
4. Peel and cut potatoes in small cubes. Add to cuajo with the remaining ingredients. Stir and cook until potato cubes are tender.

Serve alone with bread or with rice with pigeon peas. Great as an appetizer.

Chicken Gizzards Escabeche

Mollejitas en Escabeche
(8-10 servings)

Ingredients:

2 lb gizzards
3 cups water
2 tbsp adobo
1 tbsp sofrito
1 large onion, sliced
½ cup apple-cider vinegar
¼ cup balsamic vinegar

½ cup olive oil
½ jar (2 oz) red roasted peppers
salt & pepper to taste
2 bay leaves
4 or 5 cloves garlic, finely mashed
1 chicken bouillon, powder
1 tbsp stuffed olives
1 tbsp capers

Procedure:

1. Thoroughly clean and wash gizzards. Season with adobo (can be done the day before).
2. In a stockpan, place gizzards with water and half of the sofrito and cook until tender. Drain and set aside.
3. Mix the rest of the ingredients in a large saucepan, and cook for 10 minutes or until onions sweat. Place gizzards on this sauce, stir, and taste for salt and pepper. Continue cooking for five minutes more.

Serve at room temperature. Serve alone, as an appetizer, with mashed potatoes, over white rice, with green bananas or ñame.

Note: Escabeche of green bananas goes nicely with the gizzards escabeche.

Green Bananas Escabeche
Escabeche de Guineos Verdes
(10 – 12 servings)

Ingredients:

10 green bananas
1-cup olive oil
1 cup apple-cider vinegar
¼ cup of Mojo Criollo
salt to taste
¾ tsp of ground pepper
4 bay leaves

6 whole cloves garlic, cut in halves
¾ lb small onions, cut in rounds
1 red bell pepper, coarsely chopped
3 or 4 sprigs fresh cilantro
1 small jar pitted olives
3 tsp capers

Procedure:

1. Peel bananas and place them in salt water for 10 minutes. Then boil with two drops of olive oil for 10 minutes. (Or cut the ends and put them to boil in salt water until tender. Then peel them. It's easier this way and your fingers won't get stained.) **DO NOT OVERCOOK** or they will get mushy.
2. Combine olive oil, vinegar, salt, pepper bay leaves, garlic, onion, capers, olives (all ingredients) together in a saucepan and cook for 10 minutes. Stir. Let it cool. When bananas are cooked, remove them, drain and cut them in one inch round slices. Arrange them in a glass bowl.
3. Pour sauce over the bananas. Cover. You can leave them outside the refrigerator if you are using them for dinner or lunch on the same day. Eat them at room temperature.

Note: Make sure the bananas are totally unripened.

Pineapple Meat Balls
Albóndigas con Piña
(15 meat balls)

Ingredients:

½ lb ground chicken
½ lb ground turkey
½ lb ground pork
1 tsp sofrito
1 tsp salt
½ tsp oregano

1 tsp adobo
1/8 tsp ground pepper
1 large egg
3 tbsp flour
1 can crushed pineapple
1 tbsp butter to grease pan

Procedure:

1. Place three meats in a mixing bowl and mix well.
2. Add sofrito, salt, orégano, adobo and pepper. Using your fingers, mix well.
3. Add egg and mix well.
4. Sprinkle your hand with flour. Place one tablespoon of meat in your hand and form a ball.
5. Insert one piece of pineapple in the middle of the ball and cover with meat, rotating in your hands.
6. Butter a baking pan (9 x 13) and place meatballs into it. Bake at 350 degrees for 20 minutes or until brown.

Serve hot with sauce or at room temperature. Great as appetizer or as a side dish.

Note: The meatballs can be fried also.

Meatball Sauce
Salsa para Albóndigas

Ingredients:

1 (8oz) can tomato sauce
2 cups spaghetti sauce
½ cup cooking wine
2 tbsp olive oil
½ tsp balsamic vinegar
2 tsp sofrito/recaito
salt and pepper to taste

2-3 cilantro leaves, minced
2 garlic cloves, mashed
1 tsp orégano
1 tsp adobo
1 small onion, minced
1 tsp hot sauce (optional)

Procedure:

1. In a large pan, combine all ingredients and sauté at medium heat for 15 minutes.
2. Add meatballs and cook for 10 more minutes, stirring occasionally.

Note: Sauce can be prepared separately and added to meatballs when ready to serve.

Mayo-Ketchup
Salsa de Mayonesa y Ketchup

Ingredients:

½ cup of ketchup
1 garlic clove finely mashed
A pinch of adobo

½ cup mayonnaise

Procedure:

In a sauce pan, combine and mix well all ingredients.
Serve with corn fritters.

Tara-root Pastelitos
Pastelitos de Malanga
(30 servings)

Ingredients:

3 lb tara-root
2 tbsp adobo
1 tbsp sofrito

3 cloves garlic, mashed
1 tsp oregano
1 lb meat (pork, chicken or beef)

Materials needed:
Banana leaves or paper for pasteles
Kitchen string

Procedure:

1. Peel, wash and grate tara-root.
2. Using your hands, season grated tara root with adobo, sofrito, garlic with orégano and oil with achiote. Set aside.
3. Prepare meat by sautéing it. Set aside.
4. Using the same procedure for the yucca or green banana pasteles (page 88), prepare the pastelitos. Since these will be used as appetizers, their size should be small.

Serve warm with a tomato base sauce.

Beverages

The warmer temperature of Puerto Rico makes you thirsty all the time. Coffee is the main beverage and drunk any time. Coffee is given to everybody, at any age, except babies. Hot chocolate (grated chocolate) and tea are also drunk occasionally. (The tea that most Puertorricans drink is prepared with fresh garden leaves such as *paletaria, hoja de naranjo, mata de gallina, menta, yerba buena, jengibre* among others. These are often used when a person isn't feeling well.)

Puerto Ricans also prepare nutritious and refreshing drinks with the variety of fruits found in the supermarket, farmers market and *bodegas*. It's best to use the fruits that are in season to prepare drinks: *champolas, batidos* or punch. Rum can be added to some of these drinks for extra spike. One drink used at Christmas is *coquito* (a noggy drink of rum and coconut milk).

Homemade tea is easy to prepare. Wash thoroughly a few leaves (5 or 6) of mint or orange leaves, and place in a pan with three or four cups of water over medium heat. Let boil for 10 minutes. Add sugar to taste, if so desired. (Some people add milk to their tea.)

Egg Punch
Ponche de Huevos
(one cup)

Ingredients:

1 cup hot milk
1 cinnamon stick

1 egg yolk
½ tsp sugar

Procedure:

1. Boil milk with cinnamon. Let it cool for two minutes.
2. In the meantime, beat egg yolk with sugar until it is creamy.
3. Add milk to the creamy mix. Stir well.

Serve warm.

Note: This punch is often used to restore energy.

Fuit Punch
Ponche de Frutas
(10-12 glasses)

Ingredients:

2 lemons, sliced
1 bottle ginger ale
1 can Hawaiian Punch
½ qt (16 oz) orange juice
5–6 ice cubes

1 can pineapple juice
1 bottle 7up
1 orange, sliced
½ ripe papaya

Procedure:

Combine all ingredients and stir well. Add ice cubes. Serve very cold.

Note: A can of beer and a cup of rum can be added to spike it up a bit.

Spanish Hot Chocolate with Cinnamon
Chocolate Caliente con Canela
(6 servings)

Ingredients:

8 oz. sweet chocolate
½ cup water
1 tsp ground cinnamon
1 tsp vanilla

1 cinnamon stick
6 cups of milk or 1 can (12-oz)
evaporated milk

Procedure:

1. Grate chocolate.
2. Pour ½ cup of water in a saucepan.
3. Mix grated chocolate and cinnamon with water and let boil until melted.
4. Add milk and vanilla. Stir with a mixer until it boils.

Serve hot.

Notes: *1. There are two types of Spanish sweet chocolate. Read the label. If the label indicates that the chocolate has cornstarch, it will render a very thick chocolate. This type is really good with "churros" or pound cake.*

2. If using evaporated milk, make sure to mix one can of water with the milk.

3. You can add a tablespoon of rum or brandy to hot chocolate to give it spike up.

4. Since the chocolate is already sweet, any extra sugar is optional.

5. Some Spanish chocolate brands are "Chocolate Cortéz" and "Sobrino".

6. Chocolate comes from the seed of the cocoa fruit.

Banana-Papaya Yogurt Shake
Batida de Yogurt con Guineo y Papaya
(4-6 portions)

Ingredients:

1 ½ cup milk
1 ripe banana
2 or 3 ripe papaya slices
2 or 3 ice cubes

1 –8 oz yogurt (plain)
1 tbsp vanilla extract
sugar to taste

Procedure:

Mix all ingredients in a blender. If the mix is too thick, add more milk.

Note: Virtually any fruit can be used for this shake, such as mangos.

Raspberry-Banana Shake
Batida de Fresas y Guineo Maduro
(4-6 vasos)

Ingredients:

1 ½ cup fresh milk
1 banana
3 raspberries
sugar to taste

1 tsp cinnamon
1 tsp vanilla
3 ice cubes

Procedure:

In a blender, mix all ingredients. Serve cold.

Mango Yogurt Shake

Batida de Yogurt con Mango

(2 servings)

Ingredients:

½ cup mango pulp
1 cup water
3 or 4 ice cubes

1 –8 oz plain yogurt, fat free
2 tsp sugar

Procedure:

1. Blend together all ingredients for two minutes.
2. Serve chilled.

It's very refreshing. Garnish with whipped cream if desired.

Coquito
(10 servings)

Ingredients:

3 cups coconut milk (or 2 cans 13.5 oz each)   1 cup fresh milk
3 cans (12 oz each) evaporated milk   1 tsp ground cinnamon
1 can (14 oz) condensed milk   2 tbsp vanilla
½ cup sugar or to taste   1 pinch salt
10 - 12 eggs   1 litter of rum o ½ Brandy

Procedure:

1. In a blender combine coconut milk, evaporated milk, condensed milk and sugar, and mix well.
2. In a big bowl, add eggs one by one to the fresh milk and mix well. Sift and add to the blender mix.
3. Add cinnamon, vanilla, salt and rum. Mix well.
4. Taste for sweetness.

Note: A tablespoon of grated chocolate can be added for color and flavor. Use 6 eggs if you prefer a thinner liquid. (Coquito is pronounced KoKito). Serve at room temperature. Shake well before serving.

Passion Fruit with Rum
"Parcharrón"
(4 servings)

Ingredients:

5 or 6 parchas (passion fruit)   sugar to taste
2 lemons   ¼ cup of rum
4 cups of water

Procedure:

1. Open the passion fruits and take out the pulp, removing all seeds. Place the cleaned pulp in a water jar.
2. Add the juice of the lemons, water, sugar, and mix. Taste. At this point, add more passion fruit depending on how "fruity" you want it.
3. Add rum. Stir well. Serve over ice.

Note: If using commercial parcha juice, skip step #1.

Sangria
(4 servings)

Ingredients:

3 oranges, sliced
6 lemons, slices
3 cups red wine
½ cup sugar or to taste
3 cups carbonated water

1 red apple, cubed
1 slice of riped papaya, cubed
1 ripe mango, cubed
5 –6 ice cubes
1 small can fruit cocktail

Procedure:

1. Wash thoroughly oranges and lemons, and slice them.
2. Combine wine and sugar.   Stir until sugar is dissolved.
3. Add carbonated water and stir.
4. Add lemon, orange slices, fruit cocktail, and ice. Taste sweetness. Stir.

Refrigerate for 20 minutes before serving.

White Sangria
(8-10 glasses)

Use the same ingredients as above, but use white wine instead, along with white grape and one green apple.

Salads

Salads can be served as appetizers or a main course. Virtually any food is suitable for a salad: fresh, canned or frozen fruits and vegetables, meat, fish, poultry, pasta, rice, cheese, among others. Any meat used to prepare salads must be boneless and skinless. Olives and fruits must be pitted.

Be creative and let your imagination run wild in your kitchen! Leftovers can be used to prepare salads. Depending on how they are presented, they can be very appetizing to any palate. Dressings and sauces add special flavor as well as a touch of elegance to many basic salads.

Basic Green Salad
(6 servings)

Ingredients:

1 package mixed greens	1 large tomato, cubed
1 small bunch water cress	l cucumber, sliced
3 mint leaves, chopped	1 small onion, chopped
2 cilantro leaves, chopped	salt and pepper to taste

Procedure:

1. Rinse all greens and pat dry. Place in salad bowl.
2. Mix all other ingredients.
3. When ready to serve, sprinkle dressing and toss salad.

Bean Salad

Ensalada de Habichuelas
(6-8 servings)

Ingredients:

water to boil beans
½ lb chickpeas
½ lb sweet peas
½ lb faba beans
½ lb corn
½ lb black beans
½ lb string green beans

4 tsp sofrito
salt and pepper to taste
1 small onion, sliced
1 roasted red pepper, cubed
¼ cup balsamic vinegar
¼ cup olive oil
½ tsp adobo, powder

Combine the following ingredients for bean salad dressing:

2 tbsp olive oil
1 tbsp Balsamic vinegar
1 tbsp apple cider vinegar

½ tsp sofrito
1 clove garlic, finely mashed
½ tsp adobo, powder

Procedure:

1. If using dry grains, pick through them, wash, and soak in water overnight individually. (Some grains need more time than others to tenderize.)
2. The day the salad will be prepared, drain grains and add fresh water with a teaspoon of sofrito, a teaspoon of salt, and boil until tender, but firm. (Water that has been used to boil any grains can be used for boiling other grains.) Do the same with the string beans.
3. Drain grains, save water, and set aside.
4. Combine all grains in a mixing bowl. Add onion and red pepper. Toss.
5. In a separate bowl, mix vinegar, oil, remaining sofrito and adobo. Add it to the beans mix. Toss, add pepper and salt to taste.

Serve at room temperature. Serve alone, over lettuce, with pasta or over rice.

Note: *Canned grains can be used instead of cooking dry grains from scratch. Drain beans and add the rest of the ingredients. Using canned beans is a quick and simple way to prepare the bean salad.*

Chicken Salad

(6 servings)

Ingredients:

2 cups cooked chicken, diced	1 tsp black olives, sliced
¼ cup celery, diced	1 tsp green stuffed olives, sliced
1/2 cucumber, diced	1 tsp capers
½ bell green pepper	1 small onion, chopped
½ bell red roasted pepper	½ cup boiled potatoes, diced

Dressing:

¼ cup olive oil	½ tsp sofrito
1 tbsp balsamic vinegar	½ tsp adobo
1 clove garlic, finely mashed	salt and pepper to taste

Procedure:

1. Mix all ingredients for the salad in a large salad bowl. Set aside.
2. Prepare dressing by mixing all ingredients (under dressing) together.
3. When ready to serve, toss chicken salad with dressing.

Served on lettuce at room temperature.

Shrimp Salad

Ensalada de Camarones
(6 servings)

Ingredients:

2 ½ lb shrimp
4 cups water
3 cloves garlic, finely mashed
2 tsp sofrito
1 bay leaf
4 or 5 whole peppercorns
1/2 green bell pepper, diced
1 small red roasted pepper, diced
6 stuffed olives, sliced
6 pitted black olives, sliced

1 tbsp small capers
1 large tomato, diced
1 small Vidalia onion, sliced
½ stem celery, sliced
3 cilantro leaves, minced
2 recao leaves, minced
1 medium carrot, diced
1 scallion, chopped
salt and pepper to taste
½ a lettuce

Dressing for Salad:

juice of one lemon
½ tsp oregano
1 tbsp apple cider vinegar
1 tbsp balsamic vinegar

2 or 3 drops hot sauce
¼ cup white wine
2 tbsp olive oil

Procedure:

1. Devein shrimps using a small pointed knife, and wash in running water before cooking.
2. Place shrimps in a large pan with water, half of mashed garlic, half of the sofrito, bay leaf and peppercorns. Cook on medium heat, approximately five minutes. Drain.
3. Place shrimps in a mixing bowl, and add peppers, olives, capers, tomato, onion, scallion, celery, cilantro, recao and carrot. Mix well.
4. In a separate bowl, mix well lemon, oregano, vinegar, hot sauce, wine, olive oil, sofrito and garlic and sprinkle over salad. Toss and let marinate for five minutes.

Serve at room temperature over lettuce or other leafy greens.

Note: Octopus can be substituted for shrimps.

Avocado Shrimp Salad

Ensalada de Camarones con Aguacate

(4 servings)

Ingredients:

2 lb medium size shrimp
3 cups water
4 round lemon slices
2 ripe avocados
juice of 2 lemons
1 tsp olive oil
1 tbsp sofrito
3 cloves garlic, mashed

½ medium size onion, chopped
¼ cup celery, chopped
6 stuffed olive rinds
1 tsp capers
2 medium size tomatoes, chopped
½ medium red pepper, diced
salt and pepper to taste
2 cilantrillo leaves, chopped

Procedure:

1. Boil shrimp in 3 cups of water with one clove of garlic. Drain, peel, clean and cut into small pieces.
2. Combine all ingredients, except lemon slices. Set aside.
3. Cut avocados in half lengthwise and remove pit. Scoop out the pulp into a bowl to obtain avocado shells but leaving a thin layer of pulp in the shell. Sprinkle some drops of lemon over the avocado to prevent discoloring.
4. Combine the avocado pieces with the shrimp mixture. Pepper and salt to taste and add sauce. Fill avocado shells with the mixture. Garnish with cilantro. Serve at room temperature.

Tomato-Fruit Salad
(6 servings)

Ingredients:

1 head washed, dried romaine	1 thinly sliced carrot
½ tsp salt	1 ripe mango, cubed
1 large tomato, cubed	juice of 1 lemon
1 ripe banana, ½ inch sliced	1 tbsp olive oil

Procedure:

1. Break up romaine into small pieces and place in a salad bowl.
2. Sprinkle with ½ teaspoon salt, lemon and olive oil.
3. Add tomato, banana, carrot and mango. Toss.

This is a very refreshing salad.

Notes: 1. This salad should be prepared five or ten minutes before serving
any main course so that banana does not discolor.
2. Experiment with other fruits.

Sancocho, *Cocido* **,** *Asopao***,** *Sopón*

When soups, sancochos or asopaos were prepared at home, it was more to provide a hearty nourishment to those who were doing heavy physical work. These provided low cost, nutritious meals for the family. (Due to the low salaries, people did not buy meat every day. Sometimes the cook would go to the butcher/meat market and ask for the beef bones. Bones generally add a rich flavor to any soup.)

Puerto Ricans served soup, sancochos and asopaos as main dish. However, soups can be served as a light lunch or supper. With the exception of the *asopao*, with rice as its main ingredient, often the soups and *sancochos* are served with white rice. For *sancocho*, *garbanzos* or chickpeas as well as virtually any kind of meat are considered essential in its preparation.

Soup stock (*caldo*) can be prepared ahead of time by boiling beef bones or chicken pieces with bones or with the head or tail of fish in 6 or 8 cups of water. Add to the water a large onion, 8 to 10 cloves of garlic, 1 bell pepper, cilantro, 1 large tomato, salt and pepper to taste, and 2 or 3 tablespoons of sofrito and 1 piece of hamhock. In addition to preparing soups, stock can be used to flavor rice, beans, and other stews. Stock can be frozen until ready to use.

If using dry grains for soup, stews or rice, time can be cut down by soaking them in water overnight or 3 to 4 hours before starting to boil them.

Black Bean Soup
Sopa de Habichuelas Negras
(6 – 8 servings)

Ingredients:

1 lb black beans
4 cups water
3 cloves garlic, finely mashed
5 cilantro leaves, minced
2 recao leaves, minced
2 bay leaves
1/3 celery stem, cubed
1 tsp adobo
1 tbsp olive oil

3 chorizo sausages, cubed
1-cup tomato sauce
2 tbsp sofrito
½ tsp oregano
½ tsp pimienta
½ cup red wine
1 cup chicken stock
1 medium size potato, small cubes
salt to taste

Procedure:

1. Soak beans in water overnight.
2. When beans are ready to be cooked, place fresh water in a medium size pan, and add garlic, cilantro, recao, bay leaves, celery, half teaspoon adobo and half teaspoon sofrito. Boil beans a medium heat until half tender.
3. In a skillet, heat oil and sauté chorizo for about two minutes. Stir. Add tomato sauce, the other half adobo, sofrito, oregano, pepper and wine. Add this mixture to beans. Stir.
4. Add potato cubes and the rest of the ingredients.
5. Salt taste. Stir. Cook until beans and potatoes are tender.

Serve alone, with bread with garlic, white rice or soda crackers.

Note: Chorizo, chicken stock, adobo and celery can be salty. Use additional salt cautiously.

Chicken Soup
(6 servings)

Ingredients:

2 lb chicken parts
1 tsp adobo
4 cups water
2 tsp sofrito
1 small onion, chopped
4 cilantro leaves, minced

2 recao leaves, minced
2 clove garlic, mashed
1 chicken bouillon
2 medium potatoes (peeled, washed and cut in quarters)
2 ounces thin noodle

Procedure:

1. Remove fat from chicken pieces. Wash, clean and cut chicken in small portions.
2. Season meat with adobo and set aside for 30 minutes.
3. Place chicken pieces in a large pan. Add all ingredients except potatoes and noodles.
4. Let cook over medium heat for 20 minutes. Salt taste.
5. Add potatoes, stir, cover, and simmer for 10 minutes.
6. Add noodles. Cook for five more minutes, until potatoes and noodles are tender.

Serve hot alone.

Note: Rice can be used instead of noodles. In this case, use ¼ cup of rice and let cook until rice is tender.

Lentil Soup
Sopa de Lentejas
(6 to 8 servings)

Ingredients:

4 cups water
1 lb lentils
3 or 4 cilantro leaves, minced
2 garlic cloves, mashed
½ cube chicken bouillon
1 tsp adobo con sazón
4 oz cooking or smoked ham

2 tsps of olive oil
2 tbsp sofrito
1 medium size potato, diced
1/2 cup celery, diced
1 small size carrot, diced
salt and pepper to taste

Procedure:

1. Wash lentils. In a medium size pan, combine water, lentils, cilantro, garlic, chicken bouillon, and adobo. Boil for 20 minutes.
2. Meanwhile, in a saucepan sauté ham in olive oil for two minutes. Add sofrito and continue cooking for two more minutes, stirring frequently. Add this mixture, potatoes, celery and carrots to lentils. Stir, reduce heat, cover and simmer until potatoes are done, approximately 20 minutes. Taste for salt and pepper.

   Soup should turn out thick.

NOTE: *If using canned lentils, skip step 1. Reduce water to 2 ½ cups, and let cook for 20 minutes until potatoes are done. Serve with garlic bread.*

Milk Soup with Rice
Sopa de leche
(3 servings)

Ingredients:

½ cup rice
3 cups water

½ tsp salt
2 cups fresh milk

Procedure:

1. Soak rice in a cup of water for 15 minutes. (Rice will absorb water.)
2. Place remaining water, rice and salt in a medium-size pan. Cook at low heat for 15 minutes.
3. Add milk and continue cooking until rice is tender. (If soup is too thick, add more milk.)
   Serve hot.

Potato Soup
Sopa de Papas
(5 to 6 servings)

Ingredients:

3 large size potatoes
2 cups water
1 cup chicken stock
2 garlic cloves, mashed
4 oz cooking or smoked ham
1 small size onion, diced
½ stalk celery

2 tbspn sofrito
1-tsp olive oil
1 cup heavy cream
1 tsp adobo powder
salt & pepper to taste
1 or 2 cilantro leaves, minced

Procedure:

1. Wash, peel and dice potatoes.
2. In a large pan, boil in stock potatoes with garlic, ham and water.
3. In a saucepan, sauté onion, celery, sofrito in olive oil for two minutes. Add to potatoes. Stir.
4. When potatoes are fork tender, mash them with a fork or food mill. Combine with remaining ingredients. Cook in low heat for five minutes more, taste for salt and pepper.

   Serve with cilantro garnish.

"Petits Pois" Soup
Sopa de Guisantes
(6-8 servings)

Ingredients:

1 lb peas	1 tbsp olive oil
2 tbsp sofrito	3 or 4 cilantro leaves, minced
3 garlic cloves, mashed	½ cup heavy cream
1 small onion, chopped	1-cup chicken soup stock
1 tbsp adobo	1 small carrot, diced
3 cups water	salt and pepper to taste
1 small piece of celery, diced	¼ lb cooking ham

Procedure:

1. Boil peas with one-teaspoon sofrito, one clove of garlic, one-teaspoon onion, celery, and half teaspoon of adobo in three cups of water until peas are tender, approximately 20 minutes, stirring occasionally.
2. In a soup pot over medium heat, sauté ham in olive oil for two minutes.
3. Add remaining onion, adobo, sofrito, and garlic. Stir and cook for two more minutes.
4. Add peas, wine, cilantro, heavy cream, chicken stock, carrot, and salt and pepper to taste. Cook for five more minutes.

Serve hot with garlic bread. Garnish with pieces of bacon chips.

Fish Broth

Caldo de Pescado
(4 – 5 servings)

Ingredients:

2 fish heads
3 cups water
1 medium size onion, chopped
1 celery stalk, cut in small rings
salt and pepper to taste

2 tbsp lemon juice
1 tbsp sofrito
1 bay leaf
1 small carrot, diced
3 garlic cloves, mashed

Procedure:

1. Wash fish heads and place in water in a large soup kettle.
2. Add all ingredients and cook for 20 minutes. Strain.

Serve hot with bread.

Note: Variations with this caldo:

1. *For a plantain soup, grate one green plantain and add to the broth. Let cook for 10 minutes.*
2. *For a seafood soup, add 1 dozen cleaned shrimps, 1 dozen clams and mussels (washed and scrubbed), 1 lb fish filets cut in small pieces. Let boil until clams and mussels open.*
3. *Pour broth in large soup bowls and top with plain mofongo (recipe on page 86) in the center.*

Thick Chicken Soup

Asopao de Pollo
(6 servings)

Ingredients:

4 chicken pieces

1 tbsp adobo

2 tbsp olive oil

¼ lb cooking ham

4 cups water

4 cilantro leaves, minced

½ cup tomato sauce

3 sweet chili pepper

2 tbsp olives

1 tbsp capers

1 envelope sazón with achiote

salt & pepper to taste

½ cup rice

Procedure:

1. Cut chicken in small pieces. Season with adobo. Set aside.
2. Heat olive oil in a frying skillet, and sauté chicken until light brown.
3. Saute cooking ham on same skillet for about two minutes.
4. In a large pot, bring water to a boil. Add chicken, ham and any oil in the skillet, the rest of the ingredients, except rice. Cover and cook for about 15 minutes. Stir, taste for salt and pepper.
5. Add rice, stir, and continue cooking until chicken and rice are tender, about 10 minutes more.

Serve hot.

Note: *Two or three drops of red hot sauce or lemon juice will give an extra spike to this soup. This asopao can be prepared with shrimp, codfish, beef, Puerto Rican green beans, and pigeon peas, among others. A real delight in any form its prepared!*

A Vegetable-Meat Stew
Sancocho
(10 servings)

Ingredients:

10 cups water
2 pieces chicken, cut in small pieces
½ lb beef, cubed
2 tsps olive oil with achiote
3 tbsp sofrito
½ lb cooking/smoked ham, cubed
3 garlic cloves, mashed
1 corn in the cub, sliced
1 apio (root), cubed
1 yucca, cubed

1 chayote, cubed
1 green plantain, sliced
½ lb cabbage

1 large yautía, cubed
½ lb ñame
1 large batata, cubed
1 large potato, cubed
½ lb pumpkin, cubed
1 carrot sliced
1 sazón envelope
1 tsp orégano
1 can (6 oz) tomato sauce
3-4 fresh cilantro/recao leaves, minced
1 celery stalk, sliced
1 chicken bouillon cube
salt & pepper to taste

Procedure:

1. Rinse meat and clean off fat. Season chicken and beef. Sauté in oil with achiote, sofrito, ham and garlic. Set aside.
2. Wash all vegetables and roots. Cut them in small cubes.
3. In a large pot, combine water, meat, sazón, orégano, tomato sauce, cilantro, recao, celery, and chicken bouillon, and bring to a boil. Salt and pepper to taste.
4. Since some take longer to cook than the others, at three minutes intervals, add vegetables and roots in the following order:
   a. corn, apio and yucca
   b. chayote, plantain, cabbage
   c. yautía, ñame, batata, potatoes
   d. pumpkin and carrot
5. Cook until sauce is thick and the vegetable roots are fork tender. If overly thick, add more water or stock.

Serve alone or with rice and avocado.

Egg Omelet
Tortilla de Huevo
(4 servings)

Ingredients:

3-4 eggs
2 tbspns butter or olive oil
1 small onion, minced
3 garlic cloves, mashed
1 tsp sofrito
1 tsp adobo
salt and pepper to taste

½ cup heavy cream
2-3 pieces cooked ham, cubed
½ red pepper, minced
½ green pepper, minced
1 small tomato, cubed
¼ cup white cheese, cubed

Procedure:

1. Beat eggs. Except for butter/oil, add all ingredients and mix well. Set aside.
2. Heat butter/oil in a 10-inch frying pan and add egg mixture. Cover and let cook at low heat for a two or three minutes until egg mixture sets. (It can also be baked at 350 degrees for five minutes.)

Serve hot with toast or home fries. Can also be eaten at room temperature.

Banana cluster

Banana leaves

We focus attention to main meals when preparing a menu for dinner guests, which can start with a carbo base (rise or any tubers such as potatoes, yucca, among others), add meat, vegetables, a salad and a light dessert. (Health conscious eaters are reducing carbohydrates from their meals.) We also make decisions based on what we want to eat, not what is the main dish. For example, two appetizers, or a salad could be a main meal. A one-pot dish may not need any accompaniments, such as the ripe plantain pie, made with vegetables and meat. All the recipes in this book can be served as main course dishes with a few creative adjustments.

Some of the Vegetables or roots used in Puerto Rico

Malanga

Yuca

Yellow sweet potato

White sweet potato

Sweet Potato

White Yautía

Pumpkin

ñame

ñame

82

Vegetables

Root vegetables / Viandas

Vegetables, more than other foods, add variety, color, texture and flavor to meals. They are also a versatile food since they can be chopped, diced, sliced, cubed, simmered, sautéed, fried, baked, creamed, or marinated.

When selecting, storing, and preparing fresh vegetables, a few precautions are necessary: Choose vegetables that are blemish-free and at peak condition. Carefully wash (but do not soak) and refrigerate them in plastic bags lined with a paper towel. Root vegetables (*yuca, ñame, yautía,* etc.) should be stored, unwashed, in a cool, dark, and well-ventilated area.

Garlic Mashed Potato
Papas Majadas con Ajo
(5 servings)

Ingredients:

2 lb potatoes
3 cups water
1 tsp adobo
3 cloves garlic, mashed
½ tspn salt

2 tbsp butter
½ cup milk
3 tbsp cream cheese with garlic
1 pinch white pepper

Procedure:

1. Peel, wash and cut potatoes in small cubes.
2. In a large pan, cover potatoes with water, and add adobo, garlic and salt. Cook until tender, approximately 30 minutes. Drain, reserving one cup of the water.
3. Using a fork or a masher, mash potatoes.
4. Add butter, milk, pepper and cheese. Mix well.

Goes well with almost any roasted meat and a salad as well as with sauteed vegetables.

Grilled Eggplant with Codfish Stew

Berenjena a la parrilla guisada con Bacalao

(6 servings)

Ingredients:

1 lb codfish, desalted
½ tsp oregano
1 tsp olive oil
salt and pepper to taste
3 cups water (or enough to cover codfish)

½ cup tomato sauce
1 large eggplant
2 tbsp sofrito
2 cloves garlic, mashed

Procedure:

1. Desalt codfish by soaking in water in a medium-size pan or bowl for three or four hours (a day before would be even better). Next, boil at least twice, changing the water each time. (If still salty, add ¼ cup of sugar to the water and let boil for a few more minutes.) Remove bones and shred into small pieces. Set aside.
2. Grill eggplant in top of stove until is evenly seared. Under cold water, remove burnt skin.
3. Cut eggplant in pieces and coarse mash it. Set aside.
4. In a medium-size pan, mix sofrito, garlic, tomato sauce, orégano and olive oil. Sauté for three minutes, stirring frequently.
5. Add eggplant and codfish to this mix. Stir and cook for 10 more minutes. Taste for salt and pepper.

Serve with yellow or white rice, boiled potatoes or ñame.

Mashed Green Plantain
Mofongo
(3 servings)

Ingredients:

3 green plantains
3 cups salted water
1 cup frying oil
5-6 cloves garlic, mashed

2 tbsp olive oil
1 tsp sofrito
1 cup crisp pork rind chips
salt to taste

Procedure:

1. Cut the ends of plantain and place in salted water for about five minutes. This prevents staining hands.
2. Remove from salted water, peel and cut plantains in 1 ½ inch slices. Place slices in the salted water again for about 10 minutes.
3. In a skillet, heat oil and fry plantain slices until light brown on both sides but not crispy. Place on paper towel.
4. Place about six slices inside a mortar, adding half teaspoon of garlic, half teaspoon of olive oil, a pinch of sofrito, and teaspoon of pork rind chips. Press and mix with the mallet. For a more smooth consistency, add a little bit of butter and two tablespoons of the water where the plantains were boiled. Taste for salt.
5. Using a spoon, remove mix from mortar and form ball. (Decide which size you prefer: the size of the mortar or a little bit smaller.) Serve warm inmediately.

Serve with pernil, fish or chicken stock as sauce, or with ground meat sauce. The mofongo balls may be stuffed with seafood.

Note: *Mofongo tends to get dry quickly and should be served as soon as it's prepared. While bacon chips can substitute for crisp pork rind, crisp pork rind is much favored.*
For Vegetarians: Mofongo is just as great without meat.

86

Okra with Shrimp

Guimbombó con Camarones
(6 servings)

Ingredients:

2 lb okra
juice of 2 lemons
stuffed olives
2 lb medium size shrimp
1 tbsp adobo
2 tbsp olive oil
2 tbsp sofrito
½ tsp orégano
2 envelopes sazón with achiote
3 cloves garlic, mashed
1 chorizo sausage, sliced
2 carrots, (1 inch sliced)
2 cups (can) crushed tomatoes

1 tbsp capers
3 tbsp red pepper
1 cup tomato sauce
½ small onion, diced
½ cup red wine
1 tsp balsamic vinegar
2 bay leaves
½ cup celery, cut in small pieces
salt & pepper to taste
½ cup white rice, cooked
  (optional)
2-3 drops hot sauce (optional

Procedure:

1. Cut okra in three pieces each. Wash with hot water. Drain and sprinkle with lemon juice. Set aside.
2. Wash and clean shrimps. Season with adobo. Set aside for 15 minutes.
3. Heat oil in a skillet, add shrimps and sauté for two minutes, stirring constantly. Add sofrito, orégano, sazón and garlic. Stir and set aside.
4. Sauté chorizos. Set aside.
5. In a large pan, combine tomato sauce, crushed tomatoes, capers, olives and onion. Stir.
6. Add wine, vinegar, bay leaves, celery and okra. Taste for salt and pepper.
7. Add rice and carrots, stir and cook at low heat for five minutes more. Serve with avocado.

Note: Pork, chicken, turkey, beef, veal or codfish can substitute for shrimps. If using codfish, desalt before adding okra. Ham can be added for extra flavor. Rice can be cooked and served separately.

Green Banana Pasteles

Pasteles de Guineos Verdes
(25 pasteles)

Ingredients:

24 green bananas
3 green plantains
1 lb yautia
4 cups water, salted
1 cup fresh milk
salt to taste
1 cup olive oil with achiote
½ lb cooking ham
2 lbs pork meat

2 tbsp capers
¼ cup stuffed (with red peppers) olives
3 cilantro & recao leaves, minced
1 medium onion, minced
1 green bell pepper, minced
2 chopped tomatoes
1 tbsp oregano
1/3 cup raisins (optional)
1 small jar red peppers

Materials:

3-pkg banana leaves

1 pkg kitchen or butcher's string

Procedure:

Meat preparation:

1. Wash and dry meat. Remove skin fat. Cut meat and ham in small cubes. Season with powdered adobo. Set aside.
2. Combine half cup of oil and achiote, and heat at medium heat. Strain into a pan where the meat will be cooked. Add sofrito, tomato sauce, ½ cube of chicken bouillon, olives, capers, cilantro, onions, peppers, oregano and meat. Sauté for a few minutes, stirring to avoid sticking to pan or burning. Add water and cover.
3. After about 15 minutes of cooking, add potato cubes. Cover and cook in medium heat until they are tender. Set aside.

Banana Leaves:

1. Wipe leaves with a moistened cloth.
2. Then place leaves over the stove flame for a few seconds making sure the flame heats the whole leaf, so that they will soften and be more manageable when folding the pasteles.
3. Cut each leaf into pieces 10 inches long. Use one or two pieces for each pastel.

Preparing the Masa:

1. Peel off bananas, plantains and yautía, and place in salted water until ready to grate.
2. Using narrow side of grater, finely grate bananas, plantains and yautia. Add milk, salt, and two tablespoons of oil with achiote, and two tablespoons of meat sauce and mixed until is evenly colored. Mix well. Taste and add salt and seasoning if necessary. Set aside.

Preparing pasteles: (See illustration of steps)

1. Place in a small dish the olives, raisins and red peppers.
2. Using a ladle Spoon take a small portion of oil with achiote from the meat and spread on the center of the leaf.
3. Place dough with a large spoon and extend it over the leaf with olive oil with achiote. Place two tablespoons of meat with sauce in the center with 1 or 2 olives, a slice of red pepper, and three or four raisins.
4. Wrap the pastel, folding leaf to the front and the extremes towards the center. Two pasteles can be tied together or individually. The folded sides toward the center like wrapping a package. Use the cord to wrap them gently but firmly without breaking the leaf or causing the meat sauce to ooze out. To cook: Boil pasteles in a large pot in water with salt, covered for about one hour.
(Occasionally, with a long handle spoon push the pasteles on the top to the bottom of the pot, and those at the bottom to the top so they cook evenly.) Remove from pan, drain and serve hot.

Serve alone, with rice, rice with pigeon peas and salad.

Note: *a. For vegetarians: Pasteles go well with chickpeas, raisins, red peppers, olives and also with rice. Instead of using green bananas, some cooks prepare the pasteles with rice.*
b. Though not a traditional condiment, some people like adding ketchup over the pasteles when served.

Traditionally pasteles are prepared with banana or plantain leaves. If leaves are not available, aluminum foil or parchment paper can be utilized. When there are not enough banana leaves for all pasteles, a small portion of the banana leaf can be placed on top of the aluminum foil or parchment paper to keep the banana flavor. (See illustration below. These pasteles were wrapped with aluminum foil and banana leaves.) *The meat sauté should be somewhat fluid so that there is sufficient oil for spreading on the pastel leaves and helps keep the pasteles moistened.*

Grating bananas

Banana dough or mix

Meat Stuffing for Pasteles

Meat sauce with annatto oil
spread over banana leaf

Banana mix on meat sauce

Spreading banana mix

Adding meat to the mix

Dough with ingredients
ready to be wrapped

How to wrap pasteles... (*When banana leaves are not available, aluminum foil or parchment paper will fill the bill*)!

Folding leaf or paper to the front

Folding edges of paper twice to seal mix

Tuck in side ends

Tuck in mix

Fold ends toward center

Both ends already folded

Tying mid section using cord

Tying pasteles lengthwise

Boiling pasteles

An open cooked pastel

Pasteles de Yucca
(25 pasteles)

Ingredients:

5 lb yucca	2 lbs pork meat, cubed
4 tbsp olive oil with achiote	2 large potatoes, cubed
1 can tomato sauce	1 small jar stuffed olives
2 envelopes ham flavored adobo	1 small jar red peppers, sliced
4 tbsp sofrito	3 or 4 cilantro leaves, minced
4 garlic cloves, mashed	1 tbsp capers
1 chicken bouillon cube	1 box (1.5 oz) raisins (optional)
½ cup milk	salt and pepper to taste

Materials: 2 lbs banana leaves   1 package cord

Meat preparation:

1. Wash and dry meat. Remove skin fat. Cut in small cubes. Season with adobo powder. Set aside.
2. Combine oil and achiote, and heat at medium heat. Strain into a pan where the meat will be cooked. Add sofrito, tomato sauce, ½ cube of chicken bouillon, olives, capers and meat. Sauté for a few minutes, stirring to avoid sticking to pan or burning. Add water and cover.
3. After about 15 minutes of cooking, add potato cubes. Cover and cook in medium heat until they are tender. Set aside.

Masa preparation:

1. Dissolve chicken and ham flavored cubes in half cup of water. Set aside.
2. While meat is cooking, peel, wash and grate yucca. (Make sure to remove fibrous center of the yucca.)
3. After grating the yucca, squeeze out in a cheesecloth to remove some of the yucca starch.
4. Add oil with achiote, a serving spoonful of the meat sauce and the half-cup of water with chicken and ham flavored, to the yucca mix. Mix dough until color is uniform. (Use hands to mix well.) Taste for salt and pepper.
5. Add milk and the batter will be smooth.

Pasteles preparation:

1. Clean banana leaves using a wet cloth. Cut them in pieces of about 10 to 12 inches each.
2. Place olives, raisins and red peppers in a small dish.
3. Place a tablespoon of meat sauce and olive oil with achiote in the center of the banana leaf. Using a serving spoon, extend this sauce in the banana leaf.
4. Place a serving spoon of the dough in the banana leaf and extend it in a rectangular shape. Add two tablespoon of meat and sauce at the center, expanding it over the leaf. Add two olives, one slice of red pepper, and three or four raisins.
5. Wrap the pastel. Follow the same procedure for wrapping banana pasteles.

Serve pasteles alone, with white rice or rice with pigeon peas and a salad.

Note: **Chicken, turkey or fish can be used instead of red meat. The pasteles can be prepared in advance, frozen and cooked. When frozen, they will need more time to cook.**

Ripe Plantain Pie
Piñón de Plátanos
(6-8 servings)

Ingredients:

1 lb ground meat	2 cloves garlic, finely mashed
3 cups water	6 ripe plantains
¾ lb string beans	1 qt lb butter (1 stick)
2 tsp salt	6 eggs
2 oz. cooking ham	1 tsp adobo

Procedure:

1. Turn on oven at 350 degrees.
2. Prepare ground meat. (See recipe on page 103) and set aside.
3. Cut ends of string beans, then in halves, and wash in cold water.
4. Boil string beans in water, with a pinch of salt, ham and garlic for 10 minutes. Beans should be al dente. Drain and set aside.
5. Peel plantains and sliced lengthwise. Place butter in a skillet and fry slices. Place in paper towels.
6. Butter a 9 x 13 glass frying pan. Set aside.
7. Beat three white eggs with a pinch of salt and adobo. Add yolks & mix. Pour in frying pan and let cook for 3 to 4 minutes in the stove. Place slices of plantain in top of egg layer. Then place meat in top of plantain layer. Add string beans in top of meat layer, and finish with a layer of plantains covering the string beans.
8. Beat the other three eggs and spread over the top plantain layer. Bake for 15 minutes or until eggs are set. Let cool.

Serve warm or at room temperature. A salad can accompany this dish.

Note: This is a whole meal in itself and can be served alone.

Spinach with Red Roasted Peppers
Espinaca con Pimientos Morrones
(6 servings)

Ingredients:

1 package spinach
1-tsp butter
1 tbsp olive oil
3 cloves garlic, finely mashed

1 tsp sofrito
salt & pepper to taste
1 jar (2 oz) roasted red peppers

Procedure:

1. Wash spinach thoroughly. Drain, pat dry and set aside.
2. In a medium size frying pan, heat butter and oil. Add garlic, sofrito, salt, pepper and spinach. Sauté for three minutes.
3. Add red peppers, stir, and cook for one more minute.

Serve at room temperature as a side dish.

Stuffed Chayotes
Chayotes Rellenos
(4 servings)

Ingredients:

2 chayotes	l cup ground meat, cooked
3 cups water	1 egg
salt & pepper to taste	1 tsp sofrito
2 cloves garlic	½ cup cracker crumbs
1 cup cooked white rice	1 tbsp butter

Procedure:

1. Wash and cut chayotes in half lengthwise.
2. In a medium saucepan, combine water, salt, garlic and chayotes. Boil for 25 to 30 minutes until fork tender.
3. Remove from saucepan, drain and set aside.
4. Turn on oven to 350 degrees.
5. Hold a chayote in place by using a fork. Scoop out the pulp into a bowl with a tablespoon, leaving shells intact. Repeat process with the other three halves. Set aside.
6. Mix chayote pulp, rice and meat. Taste for salt and pepper. Using a tablespoon, stuff chayote shells with the mix. Set aside.
7. Beat egg with sofrito, cracker crumbs, and butter. Brush this mix over stuffed chayotes. Bake until tops are slightly brown.

Serve with salad or vegetables.

Stuffed Mashed Potato Pie

Pastelón de Papa

(6 –8 portions)

Ingredients:

1 ½ lb ground meat	½ tsp salt
3 lbs potatoes	2 tbsp butter
3 cups water	2 ½ tbsp flour
3 cloves garlic, finely mashed	3 eggs, beatten

Procedure:

1. Cook meat. (See recipe on page 103).
2. Peel potatoes, cut in halves and wash. Place water in a big pan, cook potatoes with garlic and salt until tender, approximately 20 minutes.
3. Turn on oven to 400 degrees.
4. Drain and mash potatoes with a ricer.
5. Add butter and mix well.
6. Add flour, beatten eggs and stir. Divide this mixture in two equal portions.
7. Butter a 9 x 13 glass baking pan, and place one layer portion in the pan.
8. Add meat, spreading it evenly over the mashed potato layer.
9. Add the other portion of mashed potato, covering the meat. Reduce heat to 350^0 degrees for 10 minutes. Brush some butter over the top layer of potato. Cook for five minutes more until light brown.

Serve with vegetables such as asparagus, broccoli, among others, or with a salad.

Note: Vegetarians can omit the meat and use sautéd vegetables as the filling.

Pork Chops with Vegetables
Chuletas de cerdo a la Jardinera
(4 servings)

Ingredients:

4 pork chops
1 tbsp olive oil
1 tbsp balsamic vinegar
1 tsp adobo
2 cloves garlic, mashed
salt and pepper to taste

1 medium tomato, cubed
1 medium onion, chopped
½ cup tomato sauce
1 tsp capers (with liquid)
1 can (15.5 oz) string beans
1 can (14.5 oz) whole kernel corn

Procedure:

1. Remove any fat from chops. Wash and pat dry meat.
2. Combine oil, vinegar, adobo, garlic, salt and pepper. Rub this mix over chops. Set aside for 15 minutes.
3. In a deep frying pan, sauté chops until lightly brown.
4. Add tomato, onion, tomato sauce and capers with liquid. Stir, cover and let cook over low heat for 30 minutes.
5. Add string beans and corn. Stir and let cook for 5 minutes. Once cooked, place all vegetables in a layer on a plate. Then place chops on top of vegetables.

Serve with rice, tostones, mashed potatoes or green salad.

Note: *1. If using fresh string beans, boil them separately in water, salt and a piece of ham hock. Save the liquid for a soup or sauce.*
       2. Lamb or veal can be used instead of pork chops.

Roast Pork Leg
Pernil
(10-12 servings)

Ingredients:

1 (8-10 lbs) pork shoulder	3 tbsps olive oil
10 peppercorns	2 tbsps vinegar
1 garlic head	1 tbsp adobo
salt to taste	1 tbsp dried oregano
1 chicken bouillon	2 packets sazon with cilantro and achiote

Procedure:

1. Wash meat under running water, drain and pat dry with absorbent paper.
2. Using a knife, pierce meat at evenly distributed points. Set aside.
3. Prepare seasoning paste: In a mortar, crush peppercorns, garlic, salt, and oregano, and place in a bowl. Mix oil and vinegar with adobo and sazon, and place in bowl with garlic mix. Mix well and rub on the meat and inside the pierced areas. Cover and set aside for two or three hours.
4. Turn on oven at 350 degrees.
5. In a large heavy pan, brown meat lightly over high heat. Using a shallow roasting pan, place meat in oven with rind side up. Bake at 350 degrees for at least 3 hours without turning. Baste frequently with pan juices until tender.
6. Once done, remove from oven to a carving board, let rest for 15 minutes so that juices are reabsorbed. Then, slice it.

Serve hot or warm with rice, especially *arroz con gandules*, salad and bread. Pernil can be used to prepare sandwiches.

NOTE: *Roast pork tastes better when seasoned at least one day before roasting. Keep refrigerated. When done, remove juices and set aside for gravy. Pork must be thoroughly cooked to a temperature of 350 degrees. The rind should be crispy when done. [When using a baking bag, the meat keeps its moistness since juices accumulate at the bottom. However, rind will crisp. If using a bag, pierce topside with fork.]*

Roast Pork Leg

Beef Stew

Beef Stew
Carne de Res Guisada
(6-8 servings)

Ingredients:

2 ½ lb beef	1 chicken bouillon
1 tsp adobo powder	1 small size onion, finely chopped
2 tbsp olive oil	1 tbsp small capers
2 bay leaves	1 tbsp stuffed olives
1 tsp orégano	1 cup tomato sauce
1 envelope sazón con achiote	½ cup red wine
4 cloves garlic, finely mashed	1 can beer
4 cilantro leaves, finely minced	2 cups water or chicken stock
2 recao leaves, finely minced	4 big potatoes, cut in quarters
1 tbsp sofrito	salt & pepper to taste

Procedure:

1. Cut meat in small pieces. Remove fat. Wash thoroughly and pat dry with paper towel.
2. Season meat with adobo, cover and refrigerate for 45 to 60 minutes.
3. Heat olive oil in a frying pan. Once hot, saute seasoned beef until light brown on all sides. Set aside.
4. In a large stewing pan, add oil from frying pan, add and saute all ingredients, except wine or beer, water, and potatoes during two minutes. Stir frequently. Add beef, wine or beer. Saute for two minutes more.
5. Add water and bring to a boil for about 20 minutes. In the meantime, peel, wash and cut potatoes in quarters. (If potatoes are small in size, they can be left whole.)
6. Add potatoes, taste for salt and pepper. Stir. Continue cooking covered at medium to low heat until beef and potatoes are tender and sauce is thick for approximately 20 minutes (If sauce is too thick, add water or stock.)

Serve with white or yellow rice, beans, and salad or with egg noodles.

Note: Veal or goat meat can be substituted for beef.

Chili
(8-10 servings)

Ingredients:

1 lb ground meat

2 cups (15.5 oz) red beans, cooked

2-oz cooking/smoked ham

1 tbsp olive oil

3 tbsps sofrito/recaíto

½ tsp. orégano

3-4 cilantro leaves

2 garlic cloves, mashed

1 small onion, minced

¼ cup cooking wine

1-cup tomato sauce

1 tbsp stuffed olives

1 tsp small capers

1 bay leaf

1 tsp hot red sauce

1 chicken bouillon

2 tsp chili powdered

1 tsp adobo

salt and pepper to taste

Procedure:

1. In a large frying pan, sauté ham in olive oil. Add sofrito, orégano, cilantro, garlic and onion. Stir well and sauté for a few more minutes.
2. Add ground meat. Sauté for about three to four minutes.
3. Add wine, tomato sauce, olives, capers and other dry ingredients. Stir well and cook at low heat for five minutes.
4. Add beans. Taste for salt and pepper. Continue cooking for 15 minutes more at low heat. Hot sauce can be added to your taste for extra spike.

Serve hot alone or over rice.

Ground Meat Stew
Carne Molida Guisada
(6-8 servings)

Ingredients:

1 lb ground beef	2 tbsp olive oil
½ lb ground pork	2-tbsp sofrito/recaíto
1 cup tomato sauce	3 garlic cloves, mashed
1 tbsp small capers	1 tsp orégano
6-8 stuffed olives, sliced	1 tsp adobo
2 oz smoked/cooking ham	3-4 cilantro leaves, minced
¼ cup cooking wine	salt and pepper to taste

Procedure:

1. Season ground meats with adobo and one tablespoon of sofrito. Set aside for a half hour.
2. In a large pan, heat oil. Add ham and sauté for a few minutes. Set aside.
3. Using same oil, sauté the ground meat for three minutes until pink color of meat has disappeared, and then add ham, sofrito/recaíto, garlic, cilantro, orégano, capers, olives and adobo. Stir.
4. Add tomato sauce, wine and a teaspoon of the olives' and capers' liquid. Stir, cover and simmer for 15 minutes, stirring occasionally. Taste for salt and pepper.

Note: *A.If using this meat for stuffing, sauce should be fairly thick. In this case, continue simmering until liquid is almost evaporated. If serving with rice and sauce is too thick, then add some water, chicken or beef stock.*
B. Ground meat stew may be used in different forms: for stuffing of alcapurrias, potatoes, pastelitos de malanga, chayotes, with vegetables, for chili, for omelets, meatballs, among others.
C. There was a "kiosk", behind the Faculty of Social Sciences at the University of Puerto Rico, which used to sell a sandwich called "media luna", which consisted of hot dog buns full of ground meat stew. It was the best you could eat for the bargain price!

Pot Roast
Carne Mechada
(6 servings)

Ingredients:

1 (3 lb) roast beef (center bottom round cut)
¼ cup olive oil with achiote
4 cloves garlic, mashed
salt and pepper to taste
4 large potatoes, cut in halves
¼ Spanish pork (tocino, bacon), minced
¼ lb cooking/smoked ham, minced

10 stuffed olives, minced
1 tbsp oregano
2 bay leaves
1 can tomato sauce
5-6 cloves
¼ cup red wine
1 tbsp adobo
2 cups water/stock

Procedure:

1. A day before, remove any fat, wash, and pad dry meat.
2. Using a knife, pierce meat making one-inch incisions.
3. In a mortar, crush orégano, garlic and pepper. Add salt and adobo forming a paste. Combine this paste with bacon, ham, and olives and mix well. Set aside.
4. Rub this mix over the meat and stuff incisions. Cover and refrigerate.
5. On day of cooking: Heat oil in large pan and sauté meat on both sides. Add bay leaves, tomato sauce, cloves, pepper and wine. Cook at low heat for two hours.
6. Once meat is tender, remove from pan onto a cutting board and let rest. Cut in half-inch slices.
7. Return slices to pan. Add more water until meat is covered. Add potatoes and cook at medium heat, for 30 minutes. Stir occasionally to prevent sticking to the pan. Taste for salt and pepper. Cover. Simmer until potatoes are fork tender.

Serve alone, with tostones and salad, or with rice and beans.

Steak with Onions
Biftec Encebollado
(6 portions)

Ingredients:

2 ½ lb loin beef steak
1 tbsp adobo
salt and pepper to taste
½ tsp oregano
4 garlic cloves, mashed

½ cup olive oil
¼ cup apple cider vinegar
¼ cup cooking wine
1 medium onion, sliced
½ cup water

Procedure:

1. Clean, wash and pat dry meat. Tenderize by pounding meat. Set aside.
   (Some supermarkets carry meat already pounded or ask butcher to do so.)
2. Mix adobo, salt, pepper, oregano and garlic. Season meat with it.
3. Add two tablespoons olive oil, vinegar, and wine. Marinate meat for one
   or two hours.
4. Sauté sliced onions in two tablespoons olive oil. Set onions aside and
   reserve oil.
5. In a large heavy frying pan, heat reserved olive oil. Add marinated meat
   and water. Stir occasionally until meat is tender. Add onions and stir

Serve hot with rice, plantains or a salad.

*Note: For those who prefer their steak rare to medium rare, omit water and
adjust cooking time accordingly. This recipe generally calls for a
well-done steak.*

Veal Stew with Okra

Guimbombó con Carne de Ternera
(6 servings)

Ingredients:

2 lb veal	3 garlic cloves, mashed
juice of two lemons	½ tomato sauce
1-tsp adobo	1 tbsp small capers
2 lb okra	3 tbsp stuffed olives, sliced
2 tbsp olive oil	1 tsp balsamic vinegar
2 tbsp sofrito/recaito	½ cup cooking wine
2 envelopes "sazón con achiote"	2 large carrots, sliced
1 tsp oregano	salt & pepper to taste

Procedure:

1. Wash veal with lemon or sour orange. Cut in cubes and season with adobo. Set aside.
2. Cut okra in three pieces each. Wash, drain and sprinkle with lemon juice. Set aside.
3. In a large pan, combine oil, sofrito, sazon, orégano, tomato sauce, capers and olives. Add meat and sauté for three minutes, stirring constantly.
4. Add vinegar, wine and okra. Stir and cook for five minutes.
5. Add carrots, stir and cook at low heat until meat is tender. Taste for salt and pepper.
   Serve hot alone, with rice, mashed potatoes or with pasta.

Note: **Almost any other meat such as pork, chicken, turkey, shrimp or codfish can be substituted for veal. If using codfish, desalt before cooking.**

For vegetarians:
Instead of meat, add other vegetables such as corn, broccoli, cauliflower and other root-vegetables.

Baked Chicken with Ginger

Pollo Asado con Jengibre
(6 servings)

Ingredients:

6 chicken breasts, boneless
½ cup soy sauce
1 tbsp ground ginger

4-tbspn-sherry wine
2 tbsp brown sugar

Procedure:

1. Remove bones and skin. Wash and season chicken with adobo and ginger. Refrigerate until ready to cook.
2. Combine soy sauce, wine, and sugar. Marinate chicken for half hour in this mixture.
3. Barbecue, bake or grill until done approximately 15 to 20 minutes.

   Serve with salad, mashed potatoes or both.

Chicken Breast in Orange Sauce
Pechuga de Pollo en Salsa de Naranja
(6 servings)

Ingredients:

6 chicken breasts	½ cup orange liqueur
2 tsps adobo	peeling of one orange
2 cloves garlic, finely mashed	½ tsp sweet basil
½ cup orange juice	¼ cup butter

Procedure:

1. Season chicken with adobo and garlic for about two hours.
2. Turn oven on to 350 degrees.
3. Add orange juice, liqueur, peeling, basil, and butter in a large frying pan. Sauté chicken.
4. Place chicken breasts in a 9 x 10 baking pan. Bake for 30 minutes or until chicken is done.

Garnish with orange slices. Serve with mashed potato, broccoli and garlic bread.

Note: **Some cooks add orange slices to pan for the baking process as well as garnish when chicken is ready to serve.**

Chicken Fricassé

Fricasé de Pollo
(6-8 servings)

Ingredients:

1 chicken (2 ½ - 3 ½ lbs)   4-5 potatoes, cut in halves
1 medium onion, sliced   1 cup tomato sauce
1 tsp adobo   1 tspn oregano
6 garlic cloves   6-8 stuffed olives
1 ½ cup water   1 tbsp capers
½ cup white wine   2 bay leaves
½ cup vinegar   ¼ lb cooking/smoked ham
½ cup olive oil   2 tbsp sofrito

Procedure:

1. Wash, remove fat from chicken. Cut in small pieces. Season with adobo. Set aside for at least one hour.
2. In a large pan heat oil, saute chicken until lightly browned. Set aside.
3. Sauté ham. Add remaining ingredients, except water, wine and potatoes. Cook for three minutes at medium heat.
4. Add chicken, water, potatoes and wine. Stir, cover, and cook for 30 minutes at low heat.

Serve with rice and salad.

Chicken Stew
Pollo Guisado con Papas
(6-8 servings)

Ingredients:

1 (2-3 lb) chicken
1 tsp adobo powder
2 tbsp olive oil
2 bay leaves
1 tsp orégano
1 envelope sazón con achiote
4 cloves garlic, finely mashed
4 cilantro leaves, finely minced
2 recao leaves, finely minced
1 tbsp sofrito

1 chicken bouillon
1 small size onion, finely chopped
1 tbsp small capers
1 tbsp stuffed olives
1 cup tomato sauce
½ cup red wine or 1 can of beer
salt & pepper to taste
2 cups water or chicken stock
4 big potatoes, cut in quarters

Procedure:

1. Cut chicken in small pieces. Remove skin and fat of chicken. Wash thoroughly and pat dry with paper towel.
2. Season meat with adobo, cover and refrigerate for 45 to 60 minutes.
3. Heat olive oil in a frying pan. Once hot, sauté seasoned chicken until light brown on all sides. Set aside.
4. In a large stewing pan, add oil from frying pan, add and sauté remaining ingredients, except wine or beer, water and potatoes, for two minutes. Stir frequently. Add chicken, wine or beer. Sauté for two minutes more.
5. Add water and bring to a boil. While reaching boiling, peel, wash and cut potatoes into quarters. (If potatoes are small in size, they can be left whole.)
6. Add potatoes and continue cooking covered at medium to low heat. Taste for salt and pepper. Stir and cover. Simmer until chicken and potatoes are tender and sauce is thick for approximately 20 minutes

Serve hot alone, with a salad, vegetables or rice.

Note: If sauce is too thick, add more water or chicken stock.

Spaghetti with Chicken
Pasta con Pollo
(6-8 servings)

Ingredients:

6-8 pieces of chicken
2 tbsp sofrito
2 cloves garlic, mashed
4-5 cilantro leaves, minced
1 green bell pepper, minced
2 tsp adobo
1 jar spaghetti sauce

1 box spaghetti
1 cup tomato sauce
1 medium onion, minced
6-8 stuffed olives (w/red peppers)
1 tbsp olive oil
3 cups water

Procedure:

1. Remove skin and fat, and wash chicken. Cut meat into small pieces.
2. Season chicken with adobo about one hour before start cooking.
3. In a large pot, sauté chicken in hot oil.
4. Add all the other ingredients and cook at low heat until chicken is tender.
   Set aside.
5. In a pasta pan, add salt, ½ teaspoon oil and one garlic clove to water. Bring
   water to a boil. Add pasta, stirring occasionally. Cook until al dente.
   Drain.
6. Add spaghetti to chicken, stir, and cook for a few minutes more. Sprinkle
   generously with parmesan cheese

Serve hot with vegetables or a salad.

Note: Virtually any pasta form can be used instead of spaghetti.

111

Crab Meat Stew
Salmorejo de Jueyes
(6–8 servings)

Ingredients:

2 tbsp olive oil
2 tbsp sofrito
3 cloves garlic, crushed
1 envelope annatto seasoning
3 or 4 cilantro leaves, minced

2 lb crab meat
¼ cup tomato sauce
1 bell pepper chopped
salt & pepper to taste

Procedure:

1. Pour olive oil, sofrito, and annatto seasoning in a saucepan and bring to a gentle simmer over low heat for a few minutes, stirring often.
2. Add crabmeat, tomato sauce and pepper. Cook for 10 minutes, stirring occasionally. Check for salt and pepper to taste.

Serve with green bananas, boiled ñame, mashed potato or white rice.

Note: *This stew can also be used to stuff alcapurrias, tostones, mushrooms, and other meats and fish. In addition, it can be used to prepare crab cakes. In either case, the sauce should be thicker.*

Escabeche of Fish

Pescado en Escabeche
(6 – 8 servings)

Ingredients:

4 – 5 lbs fish
juice of 2 lemons

2 tsp adobo powder
oil to fry

Marinade Sauce:

1 medium size onion cut in rings
8–10 stuffed olives (with red peppers)
1 cup white wine
1/2 cup vinegar
1/2 cup olive oil

2 cloves garlic, minced
2 bay leaves
1 tbspn capers
1 tsp sofrito
5–6 whole black peppercorns

Procedure:

1. Scale fish (if necessary), wash and cut in ½ inch round slices. Season with lemon and adobo.
2. Heat oil in a skillet (optional: Dredge slices in all-purpose flour to prevent sticking in the skillet.) Fry fish in hot oil. When browned on both sides, remove from skillet, drain and let cool.
3. Marinade sauce: Combine all ingredients and cook until onions are tender. In a bowl, pour sauce over the fried fish and cover to marinate.

Serve at room temperature with salad and tostones.

Note: *Most escabeches taste even better two or three days later. Tuna, bluefish and kingfish are the best for this recipe. They have fewer bones, are easy to filet and won't crumble when cooking.*

Basic White Rice
Arroz Blanco
(4-6 servings)

Ingredients:

1 tbsp butter, margarine or oil
1 tsp salt

3 cups of water
2 cups of rice

Procedure:

1. In a heavy skillet, combine all ingredients except rice. Bring to boil.
2. When water is boiling, add rice.
3. Stir once or twice with fork, lower heat, cover tightly, and cook for 25 minutes without uncovering or stirring rice, until liquid is absorbed and rice is tender.
4. Uncover, fluff with fork and taste for tenderness.

Note: **Some people like a brown crust ("pegao") to form on the bottom of the rice. In that case, allow rice to cook longer, or raise heat a bit longer until browned at bottom.**

Rice with Pigeon Peas

Arroz con Gandules
(8 servings)

Ingredients:

2 lbs pigeon peas
4 cups water to boil peas
4 tbsps olive oil with achiote
2 oz cooking ham
2 oz Spanish bacon
½ cup tomato sauce
1 tsp orégano
salt and pepper to taste

4 cilantro leaves, minced
½ cup sofrito/recaíto
3 cups rice
1 tsp small capers
1 tbsp stuffed olives
1 chicken bouillon
3 garlic cloves, mashed

Procedure:

1. Pick through peas. Wash and boil with one teaspoon sofrito/recaíto and one mashed garlic until pigeon peas are tender, approximately 30 minutes. (Skip this step if using canned pigeon peas, in which case use two cans.)
2. Pick through rice and rinse if necessary. Set aside.
3. In a big pan, heat oil with achiote. Add ham and bacon. Stir frequently. Add tomato sauce, cilantro, remaining sofrito/recaíto, capers, olives, and chicken bouillon. Sauté for two minutes. Add pigeon peas without water. Stir and cook for two minutes.
4. Measure 4 ½ cups of water (any pigeon peas boiled water left can be used) and add to peas. Let boil. Taste for salt and pepper.
5. Once boiling, add rice. Stir and cook until water is evaporated. Cover and cook at low heat until rice is tender.

Serve alone, with avocado, any green salad or pasteles. Preferrably serve hot, but can be eaten at room temperature.

Note: If using canned pigeon peas, use a can of chicken broth to cook rice.

Rice with Pigeon Peas and Pork

Arroz con Gandules y Cerdo

(8 servings)

Ingredients:

2 lbs pigeon peas
5 cups water to boil peas
½ cup sofrito/recaíto
3 garlic cloves, mashed
½ lb pork, boneless
1 tsp orégano
1 tbsp adobo
4 tbsps olive oil with achiote

2 oz cooking ham, finely chopped
½ cup tomato sauce
1 tbsp stuffed olives
1 tsp small capers
1 chicken bouillon
4 cilantro leaves, minced
3 cups rice
salt and pepper to taste

Procedure:

1. Pick through peas. Rinse and boil with one teaspoon sofrito/recaíto and one mashed garlic until pigeon peas are tender, approximately 30 minutes. (Skip this step if using canned pigeon peas, in which case two cans.)
2. Wash meat and cut in small cubes. Set aside. Mash orégano, adobo and garlic together and season meat.
3. Add oil to a large pot at moderate heat and sauté ham. Add the remaining sofrito, tomato sauce, olives, capers, chicken bouillon, cilantro leaves and cook for two minutes. Add meat and sauté for three minutes, stirring frequently.
4. Without water, add pigeon peas, rice and stir. Measure 4 ¼ cups of water in which pigeon peas were cooked and add to rice. Stir and increase heat to medium.
5. Taste for salt and pepper. Cook uncovered until water has evaporated. Stir, cover and cook at low heat for 15 more minutes or until rice is tender.

Serve alone, with salad, or pasteles.

Note: *If there is not enough boiling water left, dissolve a chicken bouillon in a cup of water and add it to the rice. Be attentive to how much liquid is being used throughout the whole process as the rice can turn mushy if too much liquid is used.*

Chicken and Rice
Arroz con Pollo
(8 servings)

Ingredients:

3 lb chicken
3 cups rice
2 tbsp adobo
1 tbsp olive oil with achiote
2 tbsp sofrito/recaito
6-8 stuffed olives
salt and pepper to taste
1 small jar (2 oz) red roasted pepper
4 ½ cups water

½ cup tomato sauce
6 garlic cloves, mashed
1 green bell pepper, chopped
4 cilantro leaves, minced
1 chicken bouillon
1 tbspn small capers
1 small onion, minced

Procedure:

1. Wash chicken, remove skin and cut in small pieces.
2. Season with adobo. (Will taste better if seasoned the day before.)
3. In a large pan heat oil and all the other ingredients, except red peppers. Sauté for two minutes.
4. Add chicken pieces and sauté them. Stir frequently.
5. Add three cups of water and let cook for 15 minutes. Add rice, stir and cook until water has evaporated. Stir, lower heat and cover.
6. Once cooked, garnish with slices of red pepper.

Serve hot alone, with red beans, vegetables or salad.

Rice with Vegetables
Arroz con Vegetales
(6-8 servings)

Ingredients:

1 tsp butter
1 tsp olive oil
1 tsp sofrito
1 clove garlic, mashed
1 thinly sliced scallion
1 medium size, chopped onion
3 cilantro leaves, minced
1 small green bell pepper, diced

1 small red bell pepper, diced
1 small carrot, diced
3 olives, diced
¼ celery, diced   (1 teaspoon)
5 mushrooms (optional)
3 eggs (scrambled)
2 cups of cooked white rice

Procedure:

1. Combine the butter with the sofrito in a large pan, and place over medium heat, stirring frequently for two to three minutes. (To prevent butter from burning, add a few drops of olive oil.)
2. Add garlic, scallion and onion. Stir for 15 seconds.
3. Immediately add the green and red peppers, carrot, olives, celery, and mushrooms. Stir and sauté for one minute.
4. Add scrambled eggs.
5. Combine this mixture with the rice.

Note: *This dish can be served as brunch or dinner. For breakfast/brunch you can add sausages. For dinner, the scrambled eggs can be omitted.*

Yellow Rice
Arroz Amarillo
(6 servings)

Ingredients:

4 oz Spanish bacon (salt pork)
1 tbsp olive oil with annatto
2 cups rice

3 cups water
1 tsp salt

Procedure:

1. In a medium size pan, sauté bacon stirring occasionally, until crispy.
2. Remove bacon, and add annatto oil. Sauté rice for a few minutes.
3. Add water. Stir and taste for salt. Boil until water almost evaporates.
4. Stir once, cover and simmer in low heat until rice is tender, about 25 minutes.

Serve with beans and stews.

White Rice with Spanish Bacon
Arroz Blanco con Tocino
(6 servings)

Ingredients:

2 cups rice
3 cups water
1 tsp olive oil

½ lb bacon (tocino)
salt to taste

Procedure:

1. Boil three cups water with salt in a medium size pan.
2. While water is boiling, wash bacon and pat dry. Cut in small pieces and sauté at moderate heat in a separate pan, stirring frequently to prevent burning or sticking.
3. Add rice to bacon and lightly brown.
4. Add boiling water to rice pan, stir and taste for salt.
5. Add olive oil and stir again. Cook at medium heat, without covering until water evaporates. Lower heat, stir and cover. Cook for 15 minutes more or until rice is tender.

Serve alone or with your favorite beans, any type of salad or vegetables.

Cooked Red Beans

Black Beans

Habichuelas Negras Guisadas
(6-8 servings)

Ingredients:

1 lb black beans
4 cups water
2 tbsp sofrito
1 tsp adobo
3 oz Spanish bacon, cubed
2 oz cooking ham, cubed

1 or 2 chorizos, round slices
½ cup tomato sauce
3 cloves garlic, mashed
3 cilantro leaves, minced
salt & pepper to taste
1 tsp olive oil

Procedure:

1. Pick through the beans. Wash and leave in water overnight. When ready to cook, drain and set aside.
2. In a medium size pan, combine water, one-tablespoon sofrito, half-teaspoon adobo, one clove garlic, and let them cook at medium heat until tender but firm, approximately 45 minutes. Stir once in a while.
3. In the meantime, sauté bacon, chorizo, and ham for two minutes.
4. Add salt, pepper to taste, oil and beans, and continue cooking until sauce is thick. Remove bacon before serving beans.
5. Serve over rice.

Note: *If sauce is not thick enough, add one cubed potato and continue cooking until potato cubes are tender. Be mindful that the chorizos, bacon and ham are salty. All three flavor food very nicely. However, you can omit the ham if you use chorizos.*
Also canned beans can be used instead of fresh beans.

Chickpea Stew with Pigs' Feet
Guiso de Garbanzos con Patitas de Cerdo
(6-8 servings)

Ingredients:

1 lb chickpeas
4 cups water
2 lb pigs' feet
1 tsp adobo
1 tbsp sofrito
1 chicken bouillon
½ lb cooking ham
1 tbsp stuffed olives

3 cloves garlic, mashed
3 or 4 cilantro leaves, minced
½ cup tomato sauce
1 tsp olive oil
½ lb cabbage
salt and pepper to taste
1-lb potatoes, cut in halves
2 or 3 drops of hot sauce

Procedure:

1. Soak chickpeas in water a day before. (If using canned chickpeas, omit this step.)
2. Desalt pig's feet, if necessary. (If salty, desalt them the day before. Discard the water and boil them in fresh water. Cover and cook for 30 minutes. Uncover, skim fat from water.)
3. Drain chickpeas and add to pigs' feet, together with adobo, sofrito chicken bouillon, ham, olives, garlic, cilantro leaves, tomato sauce, olive oil and cabbage. Cook at medium heat, until liquid starts boiling. Taste for salt and pepper, and add potatoes, and hot sauce. Let cook at medium to low heat until potatoes are tender. Discard any bones. Stir frequently.

Serve alone or over white rice.

Escabeche of Chickpeas
Garbanzos en Escabeche
(6-8 servings)

Ingredients:

1 lb cooked chickpeas
1 medium onion, sliced
½ green bell pepper, cubed
½ red pepper, cubed
¼ cup balsamic vinegar
¼ cup olive oil
¼ cup cooking wine
½ cup water
   (where chickpeas were boiled)

5 garlic cloves, sliced
3 tbsp sofrito/recaito
2 bay leaves
1 tsp oregano
1 tsp adobo
1 envelope *sazón c/achiote*
¼ cup stuffed olives, sliced
salt and pepper to taste

Procedure:

1. If using uncooked chickpeas, soak in water the day before. (Change water before cooking.)
2. In a large pan, bring chickpeas to a boil with two teaspoons of sofrito, sazón, and two garlic cloves until tender. Set aside.
3. In a saucepan, combine the remaining ingredients and cook at low heat until onion is translucent.
4. Add chickpeas. Cover and cook for 5 minutes to marinate chickpeas. Taste for salt and pepper.

Serve alone, or mix with pasta or salads.

Pigeon Peas with Green Banana Dumplings

Gandules Guisados con Bollitos

(8 servings)

Ingredients:

1 lb green pigeon peas (2 cans)
4 cups water
2 adobo powder envelopes
3 or 4 cilantro leaves, minced
3 recao leaves, minced
3 tbsp sofrito
¼ lb cooking ham, in cubes

1 tbsp olive oil
2 cloves garlic, mashed
½ tsp oregano
½ cup tomato sauce
4 green bananas
1 green plantain
salt to taste
1 chicken bouillon

Procedure:

1. If fresh pigeon peas are used, boil them in water with one adobo envelope, cilantro, recao and one-tablespoon sofrito until tender but firm. Set aside. (If canned pigeon peas are used, dissolve a chicken bouillon in water so there is enough liquid to cook the banana mix. The dumplings will thicken the sauce.

2. In a caldero (pot), where pigeon peas will be cooked, sauté ham for three minutes.

3. Add one tablespoon of sofrito, olive oil, half clove of garlic, orégano and tomato sauce. Sauté for two minutes, stirring occasionally.

4. Add pigeon peas and let cook in enough liquid. (If pigeon peas are dry, dissolve one chicken bouillon in water and add to the pigeon peas.)
5. Peel bananas and plantain and, grate them using fine side of grater.
6. Add the rest of sofrito, garlic and adobo to the grating mixture. Mix well and taste for salt.
7. Once pigeon peas start boiling, drop teaspoons of banana mix. Let cook for a few minutes, without stirring to avoid breaking the dumplings.

Serve with white rice and avocado.

White Bean Stew with Breadfruit
Guiso de Panapén y Habichuelas Blancas
(6-8 servings)

Ingredients:

1 lb white beans
3 cups water
3 cloves garlic, mashed
1 tbsp olive oil
½ cup tomato sauce
3 tbsp sofrito

4 or 5 cilantro leaves, minced
4 oz cooking or smoked ham
½ chicken bouillon
1 tsp adobo
½ breadfruit
salt & pepper to taste

Procedure:

1. Pick through the beans. Wash and boil with one clove of garlic until beans are al dente.
2. In a small saucepan, sauté oil, tomato sauce, garlic, sofrito, cilantro, ham, chicken bouillon, and adobo for two to three minutes, stirring frequently. Add to beans.
3. While beans are cooking, peel breadfruit, wash and cut in cubes. Add to beans and continue cooking until beans and breadfruit are tender. Taste for salt and pepper. Serve hot over white rice. Accompany with a salad or avocado.

White Beans with Pumpkin
Habichuelas Blancas con Calabazas
(6-8 servings)

Ingredients:

1 lb white beans
½ lb yellow pumpkin
½ cup tomato sauce
3 garlic cloves, mashed
3 cups water to boil beans
½ lb cooking ham
½ chicken bouillon

½ onion, chopped
3 tbsp sofrito
4-5 cilantro leaves, minced
1 tsp adobo
1 tbsp olive oil
salt and pepper to taste

Procedure:

1. Pick through beans. Wash and boil in three cups of water with one clove of garlic until beans are al dente.
2. In a medium size pan, saute ham in hot oil. Add tomato sauce, garlic, chicken bouillon, onion, sofrito, cilantro and adobo. Cook for three minutes, stirring frequently. Add beans.
3. While beans are cooking, cut pumpkin in small cubes. Wash and add to beans. Continue cooking until pumpkin is tender. Taste for salt and pepper.
Serve hot over rice. Accompany with a green salad or avocado.

Note: Canned beans can be used instead of fresh beans.

Dessert is for some people is the best part of the meal.

Which kind of dessert is served is often based on the menu. After a heavy meal, a light dessert seems more appealing, such as custards, puddings, sherbet, ice cream or simply fruits. These desserts are often more enjoyable when served in small portions. Our typical desserts can be quite sweet. One example is papaya in syrup which can be balanced with farmer's cheese or vanilla ice cream. More and more a variety of cheese and wines are being served as desserts.

In Aguadilla, my home town, we had a baker, Pilmo, who prepared the best milk candy (*dulce de leche*), the best egg custard served in a cone shaped cup (*flan de leche y huevo servido en vasos en forma de cono*), and cake (*sus bizcochitos*). He would baked them in the morning, and by midday, everything was gone. He took his recipe with him when he passed away.

My father tells me that when he was growing up, his father would prepare *dulces de paila*, which meant cooking a big amount of candy cooked in large pans or *calderos:* white sweet potato (*dulce de batata*), orange (*naranja*) and coconut (*de coco*), which were sold to support the family.

On her side, my mother and grandmother always had time to cook traditional desserts. They never waited for any special occasion. When they longed for a sweet, would simply get up, buy the ingredients and cook *la mazamorra* or *dulce de coco* or whatever they yearned for. Back then there were few ranges, ovens nor any of the modern appliances taken for granted today. I still remember that "wood" flavor that we no longer can get. Today we have the advantage of cooking faster.

Desserts

Breadfruit Custard
Flan de Pana
(8-10 servings)

Ingredients:

1 small ripe breadfruit
1 cup sugar for custard
3 tbsp butter
¼ tsp salt
1 cup flour

1 can (12 oz) evaporated milk
1 tsp vanilla
5 large eggs
¾ cup sugar to caramelize custard

Procedure:

1. Turn oven on to 350 degrees. Pour water into bottom of a double boiler (making sure water reaches 2/3 of the mold). Place in oven
2. Cut breadfruit in manageable pieces and peel.
3. Boil with salt, drain and mashed.
4. Add sugar, butter, flour, evaporated milk, vanilla and eggs. Mix well and set aside.
5. Caramelize top part of a double boiler. Melt sugar by stirring constantly with a wooden spoon at medium heat to a brown color. Coat by rotating the melted sugar in the mold.
6. Pour mixture into mold and place in oven for approximately 45 to 60 minutes, until an inserted knife comes out clean.
7. When done, remove pan from water. Place in a wire rack, covered, and let cool for 2 to 3 hours before serving. (You may serve it at room temperature or refrigerate it to serve it cold. If the custard is prepared the day before, it must be refrigerated after cooling.) Unmold to a platter before serving.

Serve at room temperature or cold.

Carrot Cake
Bizcocho de Zanahoria
(8 –10 servings)

Ingredients:

2 tbsp butter
2 cups grated carrot
1 cup crushed pineapple
3 eggs
1 ½ cup canola oil
2 tsp vanilla extract
2 tsps almond extract
one pinch grated ginger

Dry Ingredients:

2-½ cups sugar
3 cups sifted flour
2 tsps baking powder
1 tsp baking soda
½ tsp ground cloves
2 tsp ground cinnamon
1 box (oz) raisins
½ cup nuts

Procedure:

1. Butter a (9 x 13) baking pan and set aside. Set oven at 350^0

2. In a big mixing bowl, combine all dry ingredients, except raisins and nuts, which will be added at the end, after everything has been mixed together.

3. Add carrot, pineapple, eggs, oil, vanilla and almond extract. Mix well.

4. Pour mix in buttered baking pan, and bake at 350 degrees for 45 minutes or until an inserted knife comes out clean.

Serve at room temperature. Can be garnished with whipped cream.

Carrot-Corn Muffins
Panecitos Dulce de Maíz y Zanahoria
(12 muffins)

Ingredients:

1 qt lb butter (one stick)
1 cup sugar
2 eggs
2 ripe bananas
½ cup grated carrot
1 cup cornmeal
1 cup all purpose flour

1 tsp baking powder
½ tsp baking soda
1 tsp salt
1 cup milk
1 tsp vanilla extract
½ cup nuts, shredded
½ cup baking raisins

Procedure:

1. Leave butter outside refrigerator, for at least half hour before preparing mixture.
2. Turn oven on to 400 degrees.
3. Butter a 12 muffin-baking pan.
4. In a large mixing bowl, combine sugar and butter, and beat until creamy.
5. Add eggs, one by one, mixing well after each addition.
6. Add bananas and carrot, and mix well until mixture is smooth.
7. In a separate mixing bowl, mix together cornmeal, flour, baking powder, baking soda and salt. Add this mix, alternating with milk, to the egg mixture. Beat well until all dry ingredients are moistened.
8. Add vanilla, nuts and raisins.
9. Using a spoon, pour this mixture into each muffin mold and fill up to three-quarters of the way. Bake until lightly browned, approximately 15 minutes.

Delicious with coffee, hot chocolate, milk, or a cold drink.

134

Coconut Custard

Tembleque
(8 – 10 servings)

Ingredients:

4 cups coconut milk
3/8-tsp salt
2/3 cup sugar
½ cup cornstarch

2 cinnamon sticks
ground cinnamon
2 tsp vanilla
¼ cup half & half milk
(to dissolve cornstarch)

Procedure:

1. Combine coconut milk, vanilla, cinnamon sticks, salt and sugar in a 3-quart pan.
2. Dissolve cornstarch in half-and-half milk, strain and add to the coconut milk mixture.
3. Cook in medium heat, stirring constantly with a wooden spoon until it boils.
4. Reduce heat to low and cook for another 5 minutes, stirring 2 or 3 times.
5. Remove from stove and place in a platter or individual dessert cups. Let cool completely. Sprinkle lightly with ground cinnamon.

Serve cold or at room temperature.

Shredded coconut-tomato squares

Dulce de Coco con Tomate
(8-10 servings)

Ingredients:

1 medium coconut
1 ripe medium tomato
1 can (12 oz) evaporated milk

1 1/3 cup sugar
1 tsp vanilla
1 or 2 cinnamon sticks

Procedure:

1. Grate coconut.
2. Cut tomato in small pieces and soak in evaporated milk for five minutes. Set aside.
3. Combine coconut and sugar and the rest of the ingredients.
4. Cook at low heat for half hour until coconut is tender.
5. Increase heat to medium and stir continuously. Coconut will be turning to a brownish color. Keep stirring so it won't stick to pan. Add tomato with milk and keep stirring. Cook for 10 more minutes.

To test doneness scoop a small portion with a teaspoon and pinch with your fingers. If it sticks to fingers, it's ready.

Serve at room temperature.

Corn Custard
Mazamorra
(10 servings)

Ingredients:

12 cornhusks or 3 can sweet corn
2 ½ cups coconut milk
1 tsp vanilla
1 cup sugar

1 tsp salt
2 cinnamon sticks
1 tsp ground cinnamon

Procedure:

1. Peel corn and liquify grains in a blender.
2. Mix liquified corn with coconut milk. Strain.
3. Add vanilla, sugar, salt and cinnamon sticks and mix well.
4. In a medium size pot, cook at low heat, approximately 25 to 30 minutes, stirring constantly until corn mixture is thick. Do not let corn mixture to stick to the bottom or sides of the pot.)
5. Remove from heat. Serve in custard dishes. Sprinkle with ground cinnamon. Let cool and then refrigerate.

Serve cold or at room temperature.

Note: Add one tablespoon of cornstarch if cornmeal is thin.

Corn Custard

Flan de maíz

(10 raciones)

Ingredients:

2 cups cream corn   1 tsp salt
2 cups coconut milk   ¼ cup sugar
6 large eggs   1 tsp vanilla

For caramel:

3/4-cup sugar   3 or 4 drops of lemon juice

Procedure:

1. Preheat oven to 400 F.
2. Pour water into bottom part of a double boiler, (make sure water covers 2/3 of the pan). Place in the center level of oven.
3. In a blender or food processor, mix cream corn until is smooth. Strain and set aside.
4. Beat eggs lightly.
5. Add eggs and vanilla to blender or food processor. Taste for sweetness. Set aside.
6. In top part of double boiler, pour sugar and lemon juice drops. Melt by stirring constantly with a wooden spoon at medium heat to a brown color. Coat the container by rotating the melted sugar.
7. Pour corn mix into caramelized container, then place in double boiler. Lower oven heat to 325 F and place the double boiler in the middle of oven. Bake until an inserted knife comes out clean, approximately 50 mins to an hour.
8. When done, remove pan from water bath. Place on a wire rack, covered, and let cool for 2 to 3 hours before serving. Unmold to a platter before serving. (Serve at room temperature or refrigerate and then serve cold. If the custard is prepared the day before, it must be refrigerated after cooling.)

Peach Cream Cheese Custard
Melocotones Agelatinados con Queso Crema
(10 portions)

Ingredients:

1 – 8oz cream cheese
1 – 15 oz can of peaches
1 – 13 oz evaporated milk
¼ cup orange juice
2 envelopes unflavored gelatin

10 tbspn sugar
1 tspn vanilla
¼ cup sweet liqueur or sweet white wine

Procedure:

Leave cream cheese outside refrigerator for a half-hour.

1. In a small saucepan melt sugar in the peach juice at low heat. Once is melted, let cool.
2. Mix cream cheese, vanilla and milk in a blender for three minutes. Set aside.
3. Add liqueur, orange juice and melted sugar mix to blender. Mix.
4. Dissolve gelatin in ¾ cup of boiling water. Stir until completely dissolved. Add to mix.
5. Place slices of peaches in a 9 x 10-size glass pan. Pour mix over peaches and refrigerate. Chill until set. (About 4 to 5 hours)

This is a nice delicate dessert to balance a heavy meal. Pears can be used instead of peaches.

Lady Fingers Custard Cake
(8-10 servings)

Ingredients:

2 cups coffee

1 cup chocolate milk

1 cup marsala or strata sweet wine

1 tsp vanilla

1 pinch of salt

2 oz dark grated chocolate or cocoa

8 oz mascarpone cheese at room temperature

6 eggs, with yolk and whites separated

½ cup coffee licour (Kalua)

3 tbsp sugar

½ cup rum

2 pkgs. Lady Fingers cookies

1 cup heavy cream

1 tsp ground cinnamon

Procedure:

1. Prepare two cups of good black coffee and let cool.
2. In a separate large bowl, beat egg yolks with sugar until creamy.
3. Add vanilla and salt. Stir and set aside.
4. In another mixing bowl, beat egg whites until they form peaks. Fold into egg yolk mixture.
5. Beat heavy cream until it forms peaks. Fold into egg mixture.
6. Fold Mascarpone cheese in small portions into egg mixture. Set aside.
7. In a saucepan, combine coffee, coffee liquor, chocolate, wine and rum and pour some of this liquid mix in a deep platter. Lightly soak ladyfinger cookies and place them in rows in a glass baking dish (9 x 13). Once the dish has a layer of lady fingers, spread some of the egg-cheese mixture. Repeat the same procedure until there are two layers.
8. Sprinkle with grated dark chocolate and ground cinnamon over the top layer of cheese. Refrigerate for eight hours.

Serve at room temperature.

Note: This dessert can be prepared on individual glasses. Sponge cake can be used instead of ladyfinger cookies.

Milk Candy Squares
Dulce de Leche Evaporada
(4 servings)

Ingredients:

2 cans (12 oz) evaporated milk
one lime peel
1 tsp vanilla

2 tbsp clear vinegar
1 ¼ cups sugar
1 ½ cups water

Procedure:

1. Pour one can of evaporated milk in a container and cover. Keep at room temperature for three days.
2. On the third day, combine a second can evaporated milk with the first one, which by now should be sour. (This will help the candy turn out granular.)
3. Add water, sugar, vanilla and lime peel and mix well.
4. Cook at high heat. As soon as boiling starts, add vinegar and reduce heat to medium. Let boil until liquid has evaporated and liquid starts lumping up.
5. Using a wooden spoon, stir slowly without breaking lumps. When completely dried, spread on a plate and let cool. Cut into small squares.

Pineapple-Passion Fruit Custard
Flan de Piña y Parcha
(10 raciones)

Ingredients:

1 (8 oz) cream cheese
½ cup crushed pineapple
½ cup passion fruit juice
1/4 cup water
1/4 tsp salt
6 large eggs

1 tsp vanilla
1 can (14 oz) condensed milk
½ cup fresh milk
3/4-cup sugar to caramelize mold
juice of one lemon

Procedure:

1. Preheat oven to 400 degrees F.
2. Pour water into bottom of a double boiler, (make sure water will not touch bottom of top pan). Place in oven.
3. In a blender or food processor, combine cream cheese, pineapple, passion fruit and water and mix well.
4. Beat eggs lightly in a small bowl.
5. Add eggs, vanilla, condensed and fresh milk to blender or food processor. Taste for sweetness. Set aside.
6. Pour sugar and lemon juice in top part of double boiler. Melt by stirring constantly with a wooden spoon at medium heat to a brown color. Coat by rotating the melted sugar in the container.
7. Pour blender mix into caramelized container and place in double boiler in oven.
8. Lower heat to 350 degrees F. Bake until an inserted knife comes out clean, approximately 50 minutes to an hour.
9. When done, remove top pan from double boiler, place on wire rack, covered, and let cool for two to three hours before serving. Unmold onto a platter before serving.

Serve at room temperature.

Note: 1. Condensed milk is very sweet and the custard caramel is all sugar. There may not be need to use any additional sugar
2. If the custard is prepared the day before, it must be refrigerated after cooling. Leave it in the top part of the double boiler until is ready to be served. You may serve it at room temperature or refrigerate it and serve cold.

Papaya in Syrup
Dulce de Lechosa
(10-12 servings)

Ingredients:

2 green papayas	20 cloves
water to cover papaya already cut	1 tbsp vanilla
2 tbsp baking soda	one pinch salt
4 or 5 cinnamon sticks	1 lb sugar

Procedure:

1. Wash papayas. Cut lengthwise in four pieces, peel and clean inside, removing out all seeds.
2. Then cut pieces in slices of ¼ inch thick.
3. Combine water with baking soda in a large stockpan, and place slices of papaya in this water for about 25 minutes.
4. Rinse and drain papaya and place back in the stockpan. Add cinnamon, cloves, vanilla, salt and sugar. Cook at low heat, until a thick sirup is formed.

   Serve with white cheese, vanilla ice cream (or guava paste.)

Raspberry Coconut Custard

Tembleque de Frambuesa
(10 servings)

Ingredients:

1 pkg (8 oz) raspberries
1 cup sugar or to taste
3 cups coconut milk
4 tbsp cornstarch

¼ cup heavy cream
2 cinnamon sticks
1 tbsp vanilla

Procedure:

1. Wash raspberries thoroughly and place in a blender with two tablespoons granulated sugar. Blend for two minutes. Strain in a fine colander.
2. In a large pan, combine coconut milk, remaining sugar and salt.
3. Dissolve cornstarch in heavy cream, strain, and add to the coconut milk mixture.
4. Add the raspberry puree. Stir and taste for sweetness.
5. Cook at moderate heat stirring constantly until it will starts to boil. Remove from heat. Pour in a shallow glass-serving platter. Sprinkle with ground cinnamon.

When cool, refrigerate. Can be served at room temperature.

Note:

144

Coconut Rice Pudding
Arroz con Coco
(10-12 servings)

Ingredients:

1 ½ cups rice, small grain
2 cups water
5 ½ cups coconut milk
1 oz ginger (cut in 4 pieces)
30 cloves
3 cinnamon sticks
¾ tsp salt

1 cup of raisins, seedless
1 can (13 oz) evaporated milk
½ cup grated coconut
2 tsps butter
1 tsp ground cinnamon
½ cup milk
2 tsp parmesan cheese (optional)

Procedure:

1. Soak rice in water for two hours (or overnight).
2. Place sugar in one cup of coconut milk, and set aside.
3. In a small pan, combine one and a half-cup of water, ginger and cloves and let boil on low heat for 15 minutes. Strain liquid and set aside.
4. In a medium size pan, bring to a boil three and half cups of coconut milk, cinnamon sticks and salt at high heat. As soon as boiling starts, add rice and ginger liquid and cook for 20 minutes.
5. Add sugar, raisins, evaporated milk and the remaining coconut milk. Stir and lower heat and cook for 15 minutes more.
6. Add grated coconut and butter, and continue cooking until rice is tender.
7. Spread on a platter. Dust with ground cinnamon and parmesan cheese.

Serve at room temperature.

Sweet White Potato and Pumpkin Pudding
Cazuela
(10-12 servings)

Ingredients:

2 tbsp butter	6 eggs
1-¼ cup coconut milk	2 cups sugar
2 ½ lb pumpkin	1 tsp cinnamon
2 ½ sweet white potato	1 tbsp vanilla
a pinch of salt	1 cup sweet wine (e.g.
1/3 cup rice flour	Muscatel)

Syrup: In a medium saucepan, bring to a boil, for 15 minutes, the following ingredients:

1 ½ cups water	2 small pieces ginger
3 pieces of star anise	4 or 5 cloves
2 cinnamon sticks	

After boiling for 15 minutes, strain and set aside.

Procedure:

1. Butter a 9 x 13 baking pan and set aside.
2. Obtain and measure coconut milk.
3. In the meantime, peel and cut pumpkin and sweet white potato in manageable pieces. In separate pots, boil them with a pinch of salt, until tender. Drain when done.
4. Mash together pumpkin and sweet white potato.
5. Add butter and coconut milk and mix well.
6. Add flour and eggs one by one, beating well after each egg addition.
7. Add all remaining ingredients and the syrup, and mix well.
8. Place in a buttered baking pan (8 x 10), and bake at 350 degrees for one hour, or until an inserted knife comes out clean. Let cool.

Serve at room temperature. Great with coffee, hot chocolate or a cold drink.

Note: Cazuela is a type of pudding. Canned coconut milk can be used inteads of fresh coconut milk. (Cazuela is technically the pan or mold for the dessert).

White Sweet Potato Pudding
Pudín de Batata
(10-12 servings)

Ingredients:

5 lb. grated batata
3 lb. boiled pumpkin, peeled
6 eggs (beaten)
1 cup corn flour
1 cup cake flour
2 cans (12 oz.) evaporated milk

¼ lb butter
1 tsp salt
1 ½ cup sugar
1 tbsp cinnamon
1 tsp cloves

Procedure:

1. Turn on oven to 350 degrees, 10 minutes before starting pudding preparation.
2. Cover baking pan with buttered wax paper and set aside.
3. In a large bowl, combine sweet potato, pumpkin, eggs, milk and butter. Mix well.
4. Combine all dry ingredients together. Add to pumpkin mixture. Taste for sweetness.
5. Pour mix in baking pan, place in the center level of oven, and bake for 1 ½ hour or until stick or knife comes out clean.

It is best served at room temperature. Garnish with a dollop of whipped cream. Refrigerate unused portion.

Yucca Pudding

Pudín de Yuca
(10-12 portions)

Ingredients:

1 tbsp butter to grease pan
1 cup grated yucca
1 (12 oz) can evaporated milk
1 (14-oz.) can condensed milk
2 cups coconut milk (1 coconut)
1-cup cake flour
1 tsp baking powder
½ tsp cloves

1 tsp cinnamon
½ tsp ginger
4 large eggs
1 box (1.5 oz) raisins
1 tsp vanilla
2 tsp melted butter for pudding
¼ cup Marsala wine
 sugar to taste

Procedure:

1. Turn on oven to 450 degrees.
2. Butter baking pan and set aside.
3. Blend in yucca, evaporated, condensed and coconut milk.
4. Combine dry ingredients and add to yucca mix. Stir.
5. Add remaining ingredients. Stir and taste for sweetness and pour into greased baking pan. Bake at 350 degrees for 45 minutes or until inserting a knife comes out dry.

Serve at room temperature by itself or with a topping of whipped cream.

Yucca Custard
Flan de Yuca
(8-10 servings)

Ingredients:

1 cup (1/2 lb) grated yucca
1 cup sugar
1 lemon
1 can (14 oz) condensed milk
1 tsp ground cinnamon
¼ tsp ground cloves

¼ tsp ground nutmeg
1 tbsp vanilla
6 large eggs
½ cup Marsala wine or brandy
1 can (12 oz) evaporated milk

Procedure:

1. Turn on oven to 350 degrees. Pour water inside the bottom part of the double boiler (making sure water covers 2/3 of the mold). Place in oven.
2. Peel, wash and grate yucca. Set aside.
3. In a blender or food processor, combine ¼ cup of sugar, condensed milk, cinnamon, cloves, nutmeg, vanilla and eggs. Mix for two seconds.
4. Add yucca and mix well until mixture is very smooth.
5. Add wine or brandy and evaporated milk. Stir and set aside.
6. Caramelize top part of double boiler. Add lemon and sugar to the mold and melt this mixture by stirring constantly with a wooden spoon at medium heat to a brown color. Coat by rotating the melted sugar in the container.
7. Pour mixture in top part of double boiler, place in oven and bake approximately 45 to 60 minutes or until an inserted knife comes out clean.

Let it cool for one or two hours inside the double boiler. Unmold onto a platter. Serve at room temperature.

Where to find spices and Spanish cookware on the internet...

Abuela's Pique
abuelaspique@verizon.net
www.abuelaspique.net   - Hot sauce in various flavors

www.aidasseasonings. com   - *Calderos*, seasonings and other products

www.caribbeanseeds.com   - *Cilantro, culantro* seeds.

www.cheflatino.com   - Hispanic cookware and condiments

www.ethnicgrocer.com   - Herbs and spices

www.globalfoodcompany.com   - Seasonings and other foods

www.laflor.com   - Spices and herbs

www.mipatria.com   - *Calderos* and other products

www.penzeys.com   - Spices

www.sofritogourmet.com   - *Sofrito, recaito*, and other spices

www.taylorgarden.com   - Herbs and spices, organic and natural products

Cooking Terms . . .

Alcapurrias – stuffed meat patty made of seasoned, grated green plantains.

Amarillos – ripe plantains, also called *maduros* when sliced and fried.

Annatto – *achiote*, a natural food coloring

Apio del Caribe – a thick, pale yellow, root tuber, used in vegetable stews, like *sancocho*; its leaves are used to season food.

Asopao – a thick soup made with rice.

Avocado – *aguacate*, also known as *palta* in South American countries.

Azafrán – saffron, called the "Queen of all Spices" in Spain. Its deep orange, aromatic pungent dried stigmas of the purple-flowered crocus are used to color and flavor foods (paellas, soup, rice, among others).

Bacalaítos – codfish fritters and known as "torrejas" in the western part of Puerto Rico.

Bacalao – codfish. When bought dry, it's quite salty. Some varieties have bones. Be watchful when using *bacalao*.

Batata blanca – also known as *patata* and *boniato* in other countries, it has a light brown skin color, with white flesh.

Batata candela – a reddish sweet potato.

Batata mameya – sweet potato, orange in color.

Berro – Spanish for watercress.

Bollitos (Bollitas) – a type of dumpling made from green bananas or plantains, or a combination of both.

Breadfruit – *pana, panapén*. A round fruit, with green rind and starchy white flesh. Often a side dish when fried as *tostones*, boiled as potato, mashed, or baked for desserts.

Budín or pudín – interchangeable for pudding, a dessert with a thick creamy consistency. *Buñuelos* – ñame fritters: grated ñame beaten until fluffy with salt and baking powder.

Caldero – a heavy cast iron or aluminum pan or pot, in assorted sizes. Excellent for cooking rice, beans and stews.

Caramelo – caramelized sugar served as a syrup, especially for custards.

Chayote – chayote squash, a pale green or white, pear-shaped vegetable.

China – orange, also called *naranja dulce* or sweet orange.

Chicharrón – fried pork cracklings. Same can be done with chicken skin. However, pork cracklings go best when preparing *mofongo*.

Chutney – a thick sauce containing fruits, vinegar, sugar and spices and used as a condiment, originally from India.

Cilantrillo or cilantro –Spanish parsley and is the core ingredient of *sofrito*.

Cuajo – a type of pork tripe (pig's stomach)

Cuchifritos – a combination of the pig's innards.

Culantro - a long, serrated leaf, used for *sofrito* or seasoning/flavoring stews, beans and other foods. Also known as Thai parsley.

Dip – *mojo,* used for appetizers.

Double-boiler – *Baño de María* or bain Marie: a steaming method of cooking food, using two pans. The bottom one with water, and in the top one the mix to be cooked, so as not to be in direct contact with the stove heat.

Dredge – to coat lightly with flour.

Empanadas – fried meat patty or turnover made of flour.

151

Empanadillas – fried meat patty made of seasoned grated yucca

Escabeche – process of marinating cooked meat (fish, poultry) or legumes (*gandules*, *garbanzos*) in oil, vinegar, wine, and other seasonings.

Flan – custard. A double-boiler is generally used when preparing it, whether on the stove or baked inside oven.

Fold – using a spatula, the gentle incorporation of a delicate mix into another without releasing air bubbles, by bringing part of the mixture from the bottom of a bowl to the top, until all ingredients are thoroughly blended.

Gandules or gandures – pigeon peas. Can be bought fresh (green) or dry (light brown). When dry, they take longer to cook. They also come frozen and canned.

Garbanzos – chick peas. Great for salads, stew, soup, dip, and escabeche.

Granos – legumes (beans and the like)

Guineítos niños – a variety of small bananas.

Guineo - banana

Guingambó, guimbombó or quimbombó – okra. Also known as *molondrones*. Green vegetable pods used in soups, stews, and gumbos (by itself meaning okra). Can be boiled for salad, fried as a side dish, and pickled. Found in supermarkets fresh, frozen or pickled in jars.

Jueyes or cangrejo - crab meat

Julienne cut – thin sliced strips about the size of matchsticks

Kidney beans – *habichuelas rojas (marca diablo)*

Lechosa or papaya - also called *fruta bomba*. When green it can be used for jelly, and to prepare them in syrup. When ripe, can used for shakes, sangria, in juice, or fruit salads.

Malanga – taro or dasheen. There are three kinds: light brown, reddish or purplish color with purplish-brown veins. Can be used to prepare *pastelitos* as appetizers, for stews, or boiled in place of potatoes.

Mamey – mammee, a light brown fruit with yellow-orange flesh, and used in shakes, fruit salads, preserves and flan.

Mango or mangó - pronounceable as MAN-go or *man-GO*. Unripe mangos are used in chutney. Ripe ones in fruit and green salads, shakes, flan, preserves, in sauces for meats, syrup, ice cream, cakes, juices, jelly, tea, almost endless uses. There is a large variety of mangoes and, according to *The New York Times*, one of the most consumed fruits in the world.

Mofongo – fried green plantains mashed and seasoned with pork cracklings incorporated into the mix. Served as *mofongo* balls or shaped into a bowl form filled with seafood or other fillings and accompanied with some sauce.

Ñame – root of the yam family. Used for stews, fried *buñuelos*, boiled in lieu of potato.

Orégano – a very small aromatic leaf, easily grown in gardens for greater freshness. Also comes dried or ground in small jars at the supermarket.

Orégano brujo – a wild variety of oregano and used like regular oregano (for seasoning and as part of the *sofrito*).

Pan or Panapén – breadfruit

Papaya – see *lechosa*.

Pasteles – a type of tamale made from grated green bananas filled with pork meat, wrapped in banana leaf, parchment paper or aluminum foil. Lately, yucca, *malanga*, *pana* or rice can be used for *pasteles*.

Pastelillos – fried meat patty made of flour and crescent moon-shaped. *Pastelillos* are also filled with guava and pineapple for desserts when the dough is sweetened.

Pastelitos – are small tamales, made of malanga or green bananas used as appetizers.

Pastelón – mashed ripe plantains stuffed lasagna-like with meat.

Pegao – The brown rice crust that forms at the bottom of the pot.

Petit pois or sweet peas – *guisantes* in Spanish.

Pilón y maceta – mortar and pestle, used to mash and grind spices, garlic and other foods.

Piñón – lengthwise-cut ripe plantains, fried and used lasagna-like in layers to be stuffed with meat and string beans.

Pionono – ripe plantains, cut lengthwise, fried and rolled into rings and the center filled with meat and cheese.

Plátano – plantain, must be boiled or fried to be edible. The green plantains are for *tostones*, *pasteles*, soup, stuffed patties *(alcapurrias)*, *mofongos*, and must be boiled or fried. The ripe ones, when fried are called *amarillos* and can also be used to prepare *piñón*, *pastelón*, *pionono*, and as dessert (baked with sugar, cinnamon, brandy or rum), can be prepared as plantain balls filled with meat, or baked lengthwise stuffed with meat.

Saffron – see *azafrán*

Salcocho or sancocho - the words are interchangeable in Puerto Rico and describe a thick stew with various kinds of meats and root vegetables (yucca, *apio*, yams, green plantain, among others).

Sauté – to cook or brown food lightly in a small amount of fat

Scallops – known as v*ieiras* in Puerto Rico

Shrimp – c*amarón,* also known as prawn.

Sofrito – main seasoning in the Puerto Rican kitchen, composed of a variety of herbs, spices, tomato sauce, among others. *Sofrito* is fast becoming generalized culinary term.

Sour orange – *naranja agria*, used in cleaning tripe, flavoring meat, especially goat, veal, poultry, and for making mojito and orange marmalade.

String beans – *habichuelas tiernas*, also haricots verts.

Sweet chili pepper – *ají (ajíes) dulce, h*as a sweet flavor and a main ingredient in *sofrito*.

Tostonera – a gadget for mashing slices of fried green plantains.

Tostones – sliced fried green plantains with a crunchy outside texture.

Vegetables - root vegetables or tubers. *Verduras, legumbres, viandas, hortalizas.*

Viandas – tuber, root vegetables and in some parts of Puerto Rico, *vianda* is called *verdura.*

Yautía – a dark brown root vegetable, found in yellow, purple, and white flesh.

Yuca – yucca, cassave (white or pale yellow). Used to prepare *casabe*, a type of yeastless bread. Can be boiled and eaten with mojito, fried, in stews, stuffed with meat for patties (empanadillas), used as flour for dessert (pudding or flan), bread, among other uses.

ABBREVIATIONS

#	(after a number) indicates pounds
lb.	pound
oz	ounce
tsp	(or tspn) teaspoon
tbsp	(or tbspn) tablespoon
pkg	package / packette
=	is equal to, the same as

Index

References

Carafoli, John F. *Food Photography and Styling*, New York, 1992.

Clave, Diccionario de Uso del Español Actual, 4ta Ed, Madrid, 2000.

El Pequeño Larousse Ilustrado, 2002.

Miller, Paul G. *Historia de Puerto Rico*. New York, NY, 1946.

Merriam-Webster's Collegiate Dictionary, 11th Ed, 2003, Springfield, Massachussets, USA.

Simon & Schuster's International Spanish/English Dictionary, 2nd Ed, New York, NY, 1997.

About the author:

Erisbelia Garriga, Iris to her family and Eris to her friends, was born in Barrio Campo Alegre, Aguadilla, Puerto Rico. She did undergraduate studies at the University of Puerto Rico, and graduate at New York University.

Since the age of 10 she would help her mother out in preparing *sofrito* by grinding garlic with *oregano* and *adobo* in the *pilón*. For years, she has wanted to write down her mom's and family recipes. Her passion for good food led her to sit down with her parents to share most of the recipes in this book. Her brother Julio was the one who started the ball rolling for the completion of this book.